Adventures
in Prayer

Adventures in Prayer

*Using the Creative Power
of the Universe
to Change Your Life*

SHARON CONNORS

HODDER
MOBIUS

Copyright © 2004 by Sharon Connors

First published in Great Britain in 2004 by Hodder and Stoughton
A division of Hodder Headline

This paperback edition published in 2005

A Mobius paperback

1

A CIP catalogue record for this title is available from the British Library

ISBN 0 340 82670 3

Printed and bound in Great Britain by
Mackays of Chatham plc, Chatham, Kent

Hodder Headline's policy is to use papers that are natural,
renewable and recyclable products and made from wood grown in
sustainable forests. The logging and manufacturing processes are expected
to conform to the environmental regulations of the country of origin

Hodder and Stoughton Ltd
A division of Hodder Headline
338 Euston Road
London NW1 3BH

I dedicate this book to my mother and father, Ceil and John Connors, who modeled a prayerful life and first taught me the power of prayer; and to the lights of my life, my children, Ed and Jen, who have kept me praying and who make me proud to be their mom. And with deep gratitude I dedicate this book to the miracle-working power of God in my life.

Gratitudes

I keep forever in my prayers of gratitude:

Wayne Muller, who had more faith in me than I had in myself and introduced me to my awesome agent and sister-soul, Loretta Barrett

Loretta Barrett for her peerless confidence in the project and encouragement throughout this journey

My editor, Toni Burbank, a wizard and magician, for her impeccability, patience, and clarity, which ministered to me and called me higher

My treasured friend, Neal Vahle, who mentored me across the frontiers and early stages of this project

My beloved friends Sheryl Hodgins, Judi Gilford, Judie Bryla, Marguerite Romeis, and the Celebration Sisterhood: Patricia, Kim, Beverly, and Celine, who celebrated the project from beginning to end

My congregation at Unity Village Chapel whose courageous living and generous loving continually inspire me and whose stories put meat on the bones of this book

Charlotte Higgins, who held my hand and cradled my heart through the chapters of my life as the chapters of this book unfolded

Contents

Part Three

Expanding the Power

Welcome

The sky was lit up with one brilliant, larger-than-life starburst after another. It was the closing ceremony of the Olympics in Salt Lake City, Utah, and the show was nothing less than cosmically extraordinary. Multiple fireworks shot into the indigo sky simultaneously and lit it up as if the Milky Way were descending to earth. Their sparkle showered to the ground with the spectacular force of a mighty waterfall cascading into a river hundreds of feet below.

The astounding display was a tribute to the power, genius, and creativity of the human mind. But it was less than meager next to the capacity of prayer to access and display the power of God in a human life.

Prayer takes us into the mystery of God for an encounter that will forever change our lives—for the better. We can never know the fullness of the great mystery that God is, but through our adventures in prayer we create a relationship with God that allows us to experience for ourselves some of the mystery. And the more we pray the more we access this power that is beyond even our highest flights of imagination.

This book is about creating a relationship with God through prayer that is intimately personal, infinitely powerful, and deeply purposeful. It is for people who come from all spiritual traditions and faiths because prayer is a universal spiritual language. It is also for those who have little or no faith and who have, perhaps, given up on any kind of spiritual affiliation—maybe even have given up on God.

I felt compelled to write it because I have seen the power of prayer not only in my own life but also in the lives of the thousands of people I have served through my work as a Unity minister. I cannot tell you how many times prayer has saved my sanity, given me hope when I was hopeless, helped me see clearly when I felt blinded and confused by the circumstances in my life and my own feelings, healed me of deep resentments, helped me in difficult relationships, built my faith in God when I was faithless and angry with God, and blessed me with a relationship with God that makes me feel that God is my best friend.

I grew up in a tradition that prized prayer, but mostly as a way to apologize for sins, plead for mercy, or somehow convince God through great sacrificial efforts that I could be made worthy. The God of my upbringing was a harsh judge who kept score and meted out punishment commensurate with the wrong. Nonetheless, into adulthood, I continued to pray for an intimate relationship with God, one that would close the unfathomable distance I felt. I think I always wanted to love God and feel that God loved me. I never did. That is, until a brief ray of hope flashed into my hopelessness one day. The ray was bright enough and strong enough to be the beginning of a whole new understanding of God, one that has continued to bless my life.

It was late one afternoon at the end of the business day in the boutique where I was working. My friend Julie, who owned the shop, came in from the design room, took one look at me, and asked how I was doing. How was I doing? I was falling to pieces. My marriage was tearing me apart. My children were getting into trouble constantly and I didn't know what to do next with my life. Frankly, I had started to think death would be the best way out of the mess. I answered Julie's question by bursting into tears and trying, through my sobs, to tell her how awful everything was.

She said, "I know what will help. Come with me." She led me into her office, pulled a phone number out of the side drawer of her desk, and said, "We're going to call Silent Unity for prayer. Someone will ask you how they can pray with you. Don't worry about the right words to use. Tell whoever answers as simply as you can and then just listen." She dialed and I put the phone to my ear, scared and excited at the same time. A woman with a beautiful voice answered and said, "Silent Unity, how may we pray with you?" I don't remember exactly what I said or even what that soothing voice on the other end said. I know she prayed with me and as I listened I began to feel lighter, as though a huge weight were being lifted. I felt a new kind of brightness. My whole being felt clean and sparkling, like the sun breaking through an immense overcast sky. I felt embraced by an invisible energy that filled my whole being with lightness and hope and comfort.

Things began to change after that. My friend took me to her church, a Unity church, the one that this Silent Unity prayer ministry was a part of. I heard the same positive, inspiring message that I had heard in the voice that prayed with me that day in Julie's shop. I kept going back. I was a sponge, taking every class and going to every service. The message was so positive and accepting that I felt at home in a completely new and authentic way. This church was about my life. My friends and I would come out of the service saying, "I swear she was talking to me," or "How could he know? Was he eavesdropping on my phone conversations?"

I started to bring my questions to the minister, who encouraged me to pursue becoming a teacher at the church. I took every class that was offered and within a year I was teaching and leading groups.

Then one day during a workshop at the church a fleeting thought breezed through my mind: *You love everything that ministers do. You can do this.* I immediately dismissed the idea. The thought threatened whatever stability I had begun to feel. How outrageous! My family, my husband, my children would think I had really lost it. But the thought kept coming back over the next year as I continued my studies and teaching. Finally I told my minister that I was thinking about going into the ministry. She said, "I've been waiting to hear you say that."

That comment put me square at the frontier of my faith. I got an application, and as I was filling it out I put myself and God on notice, saying, "I will apply and if I am accepted I will go. If not, I will take it as a sign and get on with my life."

I was right about my family. My husband became painfully distant and the rest of my family became silent. It was what they didn't say and wouldn't talk about that spoke so loudly. At one point my father said, "I think you're making a big mistake." That was all. But I was given the courage to make that leap of faith and a year later I found myself studying for the ministry. And it all began with prayer and was accomplished with prayer. I found that with prayer, God, who seeks intimacy in and through us all of our lives, rushes into our heart with a lifting power that transforms us into a higher order of being.

Helen Keller once wrote, "Life is either a daring adventure or nothing." An adventure is a daring or exciting undertaking where we risk stepping beyond what we can control, beyond what we know, beyond what we can see, for the sake of a greater aliveness, a bigger life, a deeper peace, an unbounded sense of freedom. Prayer always leads us beyond the comfort zones of our lives. It will lead us into unknown waters, whether it's to new levels of courage or forgiveness or love. That is why I call this book *Adventures in Prayer*. In prayer we stand at what is for each of us a frontier, and there is always a certain reluctance to cross frontiers because beyond them is the unexperienced.

Prayer is an adventure because we can never predict the outcome of our prayers. It is an adventure because we learn to depend on God rather than self, and that is so unnatural to our humanness. We tend to think that we have to figure it all out, that *we* have to make things happen, that we always know what is best for us. But through prayer we come to see that these things are not true and that God's answers—even if perplexing at first—are *always* better than anything we could have imagined and produced on our own. Through prayer we open the door to discover more about God and how God loves and helps us. We can actually feel a comforting presence that is closer than breath. It took time and persistent prayer for me to come to truly trust—even though I wanted to trust more than I wanted almost anything.

Recently I heard a friend say, in response to a faith-testing difficulty in her life, "What God brings you to, God takes you through." That is part of the adventure. It's true, and the proof is in the practice. When we turn to God in prayer, we are helped by infinite wisdom to make right decisions. We are given the dreams and desires that are God's will for us, and the strength to fulfill them.

Prayer is also the avenue for discovering and developing the spark of divinity within *you* to its full potential. As in any true adventure, it takes daring to confront our fears about God and ourselves for the sake of discovering our own divinity, or what someone has called "the imprisoned splendor within." But it is the most freeing thing we can do.

What Lies Ahead

People are always asking me how to pray. First, let me say that I believe that *any* thought that is directed to the Divine, that seeks a power greater than self, is a prayer. At the same time, particular prayer forms that have been found to be especially effective have developed through the ages. This book will share many of these prayer methods with you and offer practical ways to apply them.

I begin the book by exploring what I know about the nature of prayer and why it works. I offer ways to pray that I and countless others have found effective. In Part Two I talk about the many arenas of life on which prayer can be focused, including healing, building, and sustaining relationships, finding guidance for daily living, and weathering the storms and changes of life. In Part Three we look at expanding the power of prayer so that we make the best of our lives on this earth. Here I introduce prayers for prosperity, prayers of surrender and willingness, prayers for discovering life's purpose, and prayers of gratitude and praise.

In each chapter I include affirmations and practices along with prayers. The format lends itself to small-group study and sharing as well as to your own personal spiritual discovery. I hope that along the way you will create your own affirmations, ones that excite you and support you. When it comes to praying, prayers that come from your heart are always effective. Those you find in the following chapters came from my own heart. May they be starting points for your own creativity and imagination, for expressing your ever-unfolding relationship with God.

We are, each of us, called by God to bring the invisible treasures of our spiritual character and the sweetest, most beautiful dreams of our hearts into visible reality. Prayer is our vehicle. Please join me as we journey into this adventure of a lifetime.

Part One:

Accessing the Power

In this first section I invite you to explore the idea that prayer is our access to God, to the infinite resources of the Divine. In accessing the power of God we allow it to suffuse our thinking and our feelings, ministering to us in every imagined and unimagined way.

We human beings are unique in all the world because we can engage the creative power of the universe, God, in intentional, self-evolving ways. Nothing else on the planet can. As we access this power we not only expand our own capacities, we engage the infinite resources of the universe on our behalf.

Chapter 1

Why Should I Pray?

Prayer makes one master in the
realm of creative ideas.
—CHARLES FILLMORE

Prayer helps us contact sources of inspiration and wisdom
that transcend the rational, analytical side of the mind.
Prayer provides a sense of hope and meaning—the
certainty that we are a part of a pattern that is
purposeful and intelligent.
—LARRY DOSSEY

Dear God, I give thanks today to remember that You have a plan for my life and it's a good one; and that you will give me everything I need to fulfill that plan. Gather me now to be with You as You are with me; soothe my mind and melt my stresses and quiet my fretfulness. Release me from any fears that grip tightly that I may be open to receive all that You so generously give.

The very first thing I remember saying as a child was a prayer. My parents taught me a bedtime prayer, repeating it a phrase at a time until I could say it on my own. I can't remember if I understood the words, but I do remember that saying the prayer made me feel safe and secure.

I also remember lying in bed as a young adolescent and praying, from the depths of my as-yet unrecognized isolation, for Jesus to show up in my room. I imagined Jesus as a light being. Were He to appear, I figured, it would be a sign from God that I wasn't as alone as I felt, that I wasn't as doomed and helpless as I believed. In those days, I was scared to live and scared to die.

My yearning for this indescribable relationship with God even brought me to pray that I would receive the stigmata, which our religion books said were a sign of God's special favor and special power. Looking back, I can see that mine was a beseeching desire for a relationship with God that would give my life meaning and purpose and a sense of belonging to something greater than myself. I wanted to experience a sense of oneness with God. I wanted to feel loved and lovable. I wanted to know that my existence mattered and that my life had meaning.

As I matured, my prayers matured in content but not in motivation. I still grappled with issues of trusting God. Along the way there were many sublime moments when I felt complete trust, when my life held great meaning, when I felt a great sense of efficacy and purpose. But I couldn't seem to sustain that trust until I began to pray to a different kind of God, a God of unconditional love, a God whose purpose was to plumb my depths with goodness and reveal the riches of the kingdom of heaven within me so that I might do my part in enriching everything put into my hands and path.

In all my slipping and sliding on the ice rink of faith, I have come to believe that God seeks *us* way more than we seek God and that our yearning for belonging and efficacy and meaning and purpose is actually God's yearning for us. It is this mutual attraction that is met and actualized in prayer.

Why Pray?

In the last year I started doing an informal survey of friends, colleagues, and groups I work with, asking them simply: Why do you pray? The overwhelming response was that people pray because prayer works. It gives them a connection to the Divine that they experience as help, comfort, hope, peace, guidance, and love. Some said that it gets their minds right and helps them feel at one with God and all of life. One man called prayer his direct-dial 800 number to God. He was only half joking, adding that he's learned that turning to God is always the best first choice.

Many research studies have also shown that prayer has a powerful effect on the person praying. Something potently positive happens when one human heart reaches out to the divine heart, some sort of exchange of energy that enlivens and helps the one who reaches out in prayer. (You might say to yourself, "But that's not happening for me." Just try this for a while: When you pray, whether it is a one-sentence turning to God or a longer prayer for help, be totally present to how you feel when you say the prayer. See if you can't detect some perceptible, positive shift.)

The act of praying literally transforms our moods, our body chemistry, and our habits of thought. Prayer transforms because it is both creative *and* causative. As we pray, we imbibe divine energy. In the presence of such purified thought current, our whole being is affected in healing ways. Prayer actually takes us, like a plane, out of the smog and smoke-laden air into a cleaner, purer atmosphere. Because it accesses divine energy, it nourishes our whole being. And yet there is a beautiful mystery to this most intimate connection with the Divine. Like electricity, we come to know it by what it does.

We Feel Renewed Hope and Comfort

I prayed last night with my friend Lee, who feels helpless and hopeless in the midst of her daughter's ongoing, emphatically denied bulimia. My friend doesn't know what to do next; she is afraid to confront her daughter, Teresa, and afraid not to because Teresa's beautiful singing voice is being compromised by a raw, inflamed throat that will not heal.

We prayed, piercing through the difficult emotions and painful truth, to the light of God in Teresa and to the wisdom of God available to her mom. Our prayer engaged the invincible power of God, with whom all things are possible. That prayer thought renewed my friend's hope and she felt comforted. And the thing is, in that consciousness, transformed from worry and desperation to hope and comfort, thinking is clarified and right action revealed. My friend Lee was then able to discern the next right steps to take with Teresa.

When you and I come to an all-good God in prayer, that goodness flows to us in comforting, hope-giving ways.

We Are Guided to Clarity and Right Action

Alisha had been on the verge of divorce for two years. This was her third marriage and she desperately wanted it to work but had been feeling a growing sense of discontent. She would say, "I love Tom but there is just something missing." And off she'd go on another trip—a drive to California, a visit to friends in Florida. Or she'd take up a new hobby. She went back to school, thinking maybe this would fix everything. She had even moved back to Florida, where they had met and lived for the first few years of their marriage. Tom was to join her when their house was sold. She was half hoping that wouldn't happen.

One night at dinner, a good friend suggested she do some traveling on the inside and take a real look at herself. The friend asked, "Have you prayed about how you can love Tom and be grateful for all he's given you?" I could tell she really heard this. Her heart seemed to open. I received a beautiful card from her two weeks later saying that everything had changed. She said that she had prayed and had decided to commute back to New York on weekends until the house was sold and Tom found a job in Florida.

In the wisdom of God is every right answer and right action. When we let go of all of our "right" answers and, in prayer, come willing to know the will of God, we are guided clearly and given the courage to take right action as guided. The priceless gift we receive is a stronger and deeper faith that grows each time we follow divine guidance. It is a faith not only in God but in ourselves and in others.

Peace Returns as Life's Storms Are Calmed

Paula came in just as I was leaving the office for the day. She said that she came to pick up a book for her in-home study group, which was meeting for the first time that evening. As we walked out together, she said that there was something she wanted to talk to me about. There was an unusual sense of urgency in her voice that stopped me in my tracks.

"What is going on?" I asked. As she answered her voice became shaky. "We may have to leave the church," she started. She began to explain the story, talking fast. She sounded panicky. It seems someone from her past had shown up—someone she had never wanted to see again. The texture of her emotional state was stormy. As she caught her breath for a moment, I asked if we could pray. I affirmed the presence and power of God strengthening and protecting her, the wisdom of God infallibly guiding her, and the love of God freeing her of all guilt, remorse, and unforgiveness. We were holding hands. At the end of the prayer, I could feel her hands go soft as I heard her breathe a sigh. When she spoke her voice was poised and peaceful.

God is the harmonizing energy of the universe and when you and I pray we access that harmonizing activity to minister to us in calming ways. We then can minister to the circumstance in calming ways.

We Relieve Stress by Expanding Time

Something else that prayer does so well is to relieve us, if only momentarily, of life's stresses. And of all the life stresses people complain about, the one I hear most often relates to time. No one seems to have enough of it. We feel anxious and frustrated because we don't have enough time to do all that is being asked of us by our jobs, families, and the demands of daily living, not to mention finding time for *ourselves* and the activities our hearts yearn to do. Yet at our fingertips we have the capacity to expand time.

I have gone into burnout more than once, feeling utterly exhausted, depleted, and running on empty. Many times I have found myself operating on automatic, driven by the demands of my job, without even thinking of praying for help.

Two years ago the pace of my life accelerated to the breaking point. I was sure I could not do all that was being asked of me. I had become chair of the board of trustees for our association of churches, an organization of over one thousand ministries. At the same time I took a new position as senior minister at the church at our world headquarters. I had to sell my home and leave my children, grandchildren, and friends to move across the country and begin again. The new ministry was significantly larger than my previous one and my responsibilities were far greater. So often I thought, *I can't do this.* Sometimes I felt just plain empty.

My grand finale as chair of the board came when I had been in the new ministry just six months. I was scheduled to prepare and deliver the ordination ceremony for the graduating ministers in Kansas City, Missouri, then fly to Hawaii the next day to chair three days of business meetings followed by three days of board meetings, then give both a keynote and a farewell address as outgoing chair.

I began to feel a sense of panic at the thought of all I had to prepare in such a short time. There was no way I could get it all done. Until I remembered to pray.

Recalling all the ways prayer had helped me in the past, I decided to practice believing that God would help me with this too. Each time I sat down to prepare for a meeting or speech, I gave thanks to God for the miracle of expanded time. I also thanked God for the chance to do all these great things. I reminded myself that even if I didn't think I was up to accomplishing them, God surely was. I prayed for wisdom and guidance and creative ideas.

What happened next was extraordinary. All kinds of creative ideas started flowing through me. I was able to prepare everything I needed without struggling or working into the wee hours of the morning. Time just seemed to expand.

After the conference, many people thanked me for the way I guided the meetings and told me that they were blessed by my presentations. But I know it wasn't my own doing. It was a power much greater than myself working through me and for me.

This experience caused a quantum shift in my thinking, as I had *actually experienced* time expanding. The fear of failure that had for so long plagued me and stopped me from doing the things I longed to do all but dissolved. I came to believe that I could do more than I had ever thought possible. I could say yes to opportunities and still have balance in my life. What I discovered through prayer is that time is not the issue; it is only our beliefs about time and the source of creative energy that get in our way.

You see, prayer takes you into the realms of limitlessness in every arena of your life. Instead of saying "I can't because . . ." you will find yourself saying, "With God all things are possible."

Our Relationship with God, Ourselves, and Others Is Strengthened

I prayed my way to a God I could trust, something I had always wanted but never really had. It took time and experience in following the guidance I received in prayer; many times praying for strength and courage to do something I was afraid to do, and then doing it; letting go of obsessing about and standing in the unknown, letting God be in charge of the way things went.

One of my spiritual teachers suggested, "Start trusting God in little things." I did. I asked for guidance in little decisions of the day. I asked for the right words to say in nonthreatening conversations first, then the more difficult ones. Along the way I began to notice that I not only came to trust God more, I actually began to trust myself more. And, because I trusted myself more, I discovered that I could be more trusting of others.

I have heard many recovering alcoholics say that, in the beginning, they didn't even want to hear the word *God*. Nevertheless, they followed the suggestion that they start their day in prayer, asking God to guide their day. Over time they noticed how much better their days went when they prayed. A deep trust began to develop, a trust so deep that they were given the power to clean up their past, heal broken relationships, and lead satisfying, productive lives.

In prayer, the confusion and lack of clarity that arise from the polarities of our humanness—right and wrong, kind and unkind, secure and insecure—are poured into the chalice of the Divine, where they are interpenetrated by divine energy. A kind of alchemy takes place in which the raw iron of our hearts is transformed into the gold of trust and radical optimism. We come to feel a sense of belonging and being at home in our own skin and in the universe. This relationship with the Divine is truly the marriage made in heaven and is the hope that gives us a reason to pray. When that relationship gets right, all other relationships begin to be righted.

It doesn't come easy, though. Like any vibrant, rewarding, and fulfilling relationship it takes a passion for the possible and a commitment to the practices that build trusting relationships.

We Become God's Instruments in the World

As we surrender to a full-bodied relationship with God through prayer—and to the feelings of irrepressible joy, authentic freedom of being, and indestructible hope that then blossom within us—God begins to use us to heal and bless the world. We become God's instrument, touching the hearts of others in healing, bonding ways.

A dear friend of mine named Ann was a self-described hopeless alcoholic. She always did well in school, was actually brilliant, but her personal life was a mess. She was in and out of treatment centers and in and out of marriages. Finally, she prayed for help, asking the obsession with drink to be removed. She got herself into Alcoholics Anonymous and began, for the first time, to follow the suggestions. That alone is amazing enough. God used her to help many other women find sobriety as well. Just as amazing and inspiring was her unshakable sobriety and incredible resilience in the face of serious physical problems.

After being sober for ten years, she underwent an amputation of one of her legs from the knee down. She would not be defeated by this and began taking flying lessons, becoming a small-aircraft pilot. In the coming years she had major surgeries for one thing after another—her other leg, hip, shoulder, teeth.

I never heard her complain once. She would admit that it was difficult, that her faith was sometimes shaken. But it never shattered because her God was good and always gave her the strength she needed. Prayer was a way of life for her. She said to me more than once, "You never know how big your faith is until it gets tested."

Her courage and faith in God made her a sought-after speaker in AA circles. Her light was a beacon for others who desperately needed hope for their own lives.

One day on the hills of Galilee, Jesus said the most astonishing thing to the people who had gathered in hopes of hearing him teach. What he told them was more than helpful. It was life-changing. He said, "You are the light of the world . . . let your light shine so that people can see the good things you do and give glory to God." He was telling them that they were to be the presence of God for the world; that they were to let the light of goodness and love shine through them so that others might be inspired to believe in their own light.

That message is for each of us. Jesus was saying that finding God's light in us and letting it shine not only makes our own lives better but contributes to making others' lives better. My friend Ann was an incredible light in the world. I am quite sure she was instrumental in enriching countless others' lives. I know she enriched mine tremendously.

I have another friend, Len, who struggled with his weight for years—up and down, always a roller-coaster ride emotionally and physically. When he finally surrendered to a power greater than himself and began to pray this power into his eating habits, things changed dramatically. He changed dramatically. Len and I were talking about the whole thing one day and he summed it up by saying, "God takes our greatest difficulty and turns it into our greatest strength, which becomes our marketable essence for which the world richly rewards us and by which we make our contribution to the world."

In prayer we enter into a true partnership with the Divine that helps us fashion the kind of life we truly want to live and makes us an instrument for good in the world.

We Become Blessed with Life-Enhancing Energy

Prayer is an energy that, like oxygen, feeds our whole being even when we are not aware of it. When we pray, a positive, life-enhancing energy that affects us physically, emotionally, intellectually, and spiritually is activated within us. Prayer ministers to us. It engages the creative energy of the universe, God. This divine energy unites with our own deepest, truest intention and goes into action. We ingest a higher, more refined kind of thinking, and this higher vibration brings its nutrients to our whole being. It is like the effect that eating healthier foods has on the body and on our sense of well-being. When we eat healthier, we feel healthier. The same is true of our thinking. Even when we are not aware of prayer's dynamic activity, it is at work in us and through us.

My friend Maria found herself feeling depressed often. She was having trouble in her friendships and a lot of conflict in her marriage. We talked about the possibility of her finding a spiritual home, a church that would feed her spirit. She decided to go back to a church she had been attending and even joined a morning prayer group.

I soon noticed a significant change. Maria began to develop a relationship with God that gave her a new way of looking at herself, her life, and her relationships. The tearful, desperate phone calls stopped. Instead I would hear a bright, optimistic voice on the other end of the phone line. She talked about how she came to ask God for help in difficult moments. She said, "Sometimes I just go over to the Bible and open it up. I read a little and ask God to help me. I calm down and God seems to take my anger and I feel better." She found the spiritual truth that through prayer, God will do for us what we cannot do for ourselves.

Whenever I pray with people, whether in person or over the phone, we both invariably notice a shift in energy. Where there may have been agitation, there is calm. Where there was fear, there comes hope. This is because when we think about God, we get our minds off the problem and onto the solution. Prayer focuses our attention on the truth that God is personal and is a present help no matter what the circumstance.

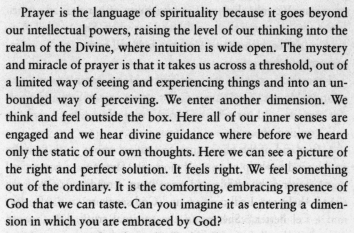

Random Readings

Many people use this simple practice whenever they feel the need for spiritual reassurance or guidance. Say a simple prayer like, "God, show me what You want me to know." Then simply open the Bible to any page and read the passage (or portion) you find there. Breathe in and think about what God might be saying to you through this so-called random reading.

Prayer is the language of spirituality because it goes beyond our intellectual powers, raising the level of our thinking into the realm of the Divine, where intuition is wide open. The mystery and miracle of prayer is that it takes us across a threshold, out of a limited way of seeing and experiencing things and into an unbounded way of perceiving. We enter another dimension. We think and feel outside the box. Here all of our inner senses are engaged and we hear divine guidance where before we heard only the static of our own thoughts. Here we can see a picture of the right and perfect solution. It feels right. We feel something out of the ordinary. It is the comforting, embracing presence of God that we can taste. Can you imagine it as entering a dimension in which you are embraced by God?

As you respond to the seeking of God in prayer, over time you will be transformed even at the cellular level. Whether a prayer of entreaty, praise, or gratitude, no matter what its emotional tone, prayer is our very soul bridging a perception of distance to the Divine. It is the self-awareness of being a wave in the ocean of the Divine.

Five Spiritual Principles:
Foundations for Effective Prayer

Many years ago a friend invited me to a class at her church where I was introduced to five of the most life-changing, spiritual teachings I know. They are congruent with the teachings of Jesus as well as the other spiritual masters of all time, and they form the foundation for focusing and expanding the power of prayer that you will find in the succeeding chapters. I found that as I practiced believing and praying from these ideas, my prayers seemed to be more effective. These ideas not only changed the way I prayed, they changed the soul I was praying from. I ask you to open your heart to them and try them on—one prayer at a time.

1. *God is Goodness and Creativity itself, seeking expression through us.*

I remember one of my spiritual mentors saying to me one evening, "If you don't have a God you like, create one and act as if it were true." I was shocked by the idea at first, but I couldn't stop thinking about it.

I decided I didn't have much to lose by trying on this totally new idea about God. The God of my childhood faith was a God that I didn't really trust, and I wasn't sure at all that He liked me either. In fact, I had stacked up evidence that He didn't. But maybe I could simply change my picture of God. And that would mean figuring out what kind of God I wanted. What a wonderful assignment!

I decided I wanted a God who was loving, caring, and present to me . . . a God I could count on no matter what. And so I began to act as if this were true. This "acting as if" was the beginning of what has become the most wonderful, intimate relationship I have ever known. Believe me, I never imagined I'd be saying that God is my best friend, but it's true!

By praying from the belief that God is a potential good waiting to happen, I gave great power to my prayers. Instead of praying with a worried, tentative mind, I began praying with great hope, and this in itself was life transforming.

I've known people who have literally run from the word *God*. Just mention it and they're out of here. They wanted nothing to do with the punishing and capricious God of their upbringing.

I've also heard many names for God, from those of the world's faith traditions, from cosmologists and quantum physicists, from the agnostic and the aspiring, from the devout and the disillusioned. The word we use is not the key here. The important thing is to come to believe in a presence and power that is all-good, that is personal as well as a principle.

What is important is to come to believe in a God you can count on to care for and be present for you, right where you are, right now and in every moment, no matter how bad, difficult, or painful your situation may be. Try it. Imagine the kind of God you want and begin to act as if it's fact. Then watch and see what happens.

2. *We are made in the image and likeness of God.*

We actually contain the essence of the Divine. How could it be otherwise? How could we be essentially different from the One who made us? We can misunderstand and misinterpret who we really are, but we can't change the truth. This seed of the Divine inheres in our very being with infinite potential and possibilities for good and abides in us as our gifts and talents, our soul yearnings, and our deepest desires—all of which are discovered and developed through prayer.

Michelangelo explained the way he created his masterpieces by saying that the figures he sculpted already existed in the marble. He simply chipped away at everything that was not that figure.

The same is true for you. This divine character lives in you and prayer helps chip away at what is not that character.

Through working with the next three principles, we succeed in sculpting the magnificent work of art that we are.

3. What we think about we bring about.

In other words, thought is both creative and causative. What we give our attention to creates our experience. This principle is one of the most elegantly simple and most powerful truths in the universe. It is the law of creation. Everything that exists came out of the void, first as an idea, then as a manifestation of the idea.

This creative law brought the universe into being. In the first book of the Bible, it is beautifully described by saying, "In the beginning . . . the earth was without form and void and darkness was on the face of the deep. And the Spirit of God was hovering over the face of the waters and God said, Let there be light and there was light." As the Creator of the universe brought form out of the deep void, we bring form out of our own depths. The light of an idea breaks through the darkness of the unknown. The same is true for every invention. It is always first an idea in the mind of the inventor.

This is the law by which we bring our ideas into expression. We create according to the patterns of our thinking. The key is to focus our thinking on what we *want* to create rather than on what we *don't* want to create; worrying, for example, can be viewed as praying for what we don't want. The law always works, whether or not we are consciously aware of it or believe it. I've heard it said that we can't break the law; we can only break ourselves against it.

Thoughts or words of resentment, greed, intolerance, self-deprecation, jealousy—these draw more experiences of their kind, more reasons to feel that way. They produce what we don't want—feelings of inadequacy, alienation, and lack. Likewise, thoughts of gratitude, appreciation, love, and acceptance draw these kind of experiences into our lives. In Scripture, Paul suggests that we focus our thinking on whatever is noble, pure, praiseworthy, and good. He adds that the reward for such effort is the peace of God, which passes all understanding.

When we let this truth guide our thinking, choosing our thoughts with care and intention, we create much more satisfying experiences and build the life we deeply desire and yearn for.

4. *Affirmation is our creative energy; denial is our spiritual eraser.*

Drawing on the law of creation, this fourth principle focuses our thinking on what we want to create and dissolves those beliefs and perceptions that we recognize as self-defeating. The twin spiritual tools of affirmation and denial are our yes- and nay-saying powers.

Denial is our spiritual eraser, releasing us from any thoughts that do not enhance our life and sense of well-being. Affirmation is the creator, the builder of the life we dream of. It puts our faith to its right work of constructing a meaningful and happy life.

Denial and affirmation play a central role in all effective prayer. When you pray, all your erroneous beliefs and perceptions will come bubbling up. For example, when praying for the right and perfect employment, work that makes your heart sing, all of the reasons why you won't be able to find it will come up: the market is flooded, the economy is off, you don't have the right skills. Fill in the blanks. Denial is the prayer activity of *releasing* these unhelpful thoughts. With affirmations you build the belief that perfect, meaningful work is there for you. As you come to believe, you open yourself to the infinite possibilities available to you. You open yourself to the always-present and available guidance of

Spirit. As you release debilitating thoughts and anchor positive, encouraging thoughts, you are strengthened to overcome obstacles and move through difficulties. You are building spiritual muscle.

You actually become magnetic to opportunity, sending out currents of energy that draw you to it and it to you.

Using affirmation and denial takes vigilance; you have to be willing to manage your moment-to-moment thoughts and choose what to feed and what to release. At first it may seem tedious, but with time it becomes almost effortless. Remember learning to ride a bike or swim or play a musical instrument? At first you felt awkward and unsure, but with practice you could do it with ease, as if you had been doing it all your life. That's the way it is with paying attention to your thoughts and deciding which to feed and which to starve: in time it becomes almost second nature.

5. Prayer and meditation access all of the resources of Spirit.

In prayer, we focus our thoughts on God, seek God's presence as an experience. Prayer is our reaching out to touch and be touched by God. It is tuning in the frequency of our mind to God. We make ourselves open and receptive.

In meditation, we endeavor to still our thoughts and enter a space where there is a sacred silence. In the practice of prayer we make the connection to the invisible, yet immediately present, realm of spirit—the activity of God. In prayer, we actually connect at some level with God's yearning in us. When we then enter the silence of meditation, whether it be for brief moments, many minutes, or even hours, we make ourselves available to hearing, feeling, and tasting God's response in us. God is always there, but we aren't. In the internal silence the peace of God flourishes.

Meditation isn't complicated but it does take discipline. Quieting our thoughts is not an easy task. Our creative minds are like two-year-olds that just don't know how to stop. Like little children, they don't want to take a nap. God ministers to us, replenishes us in times of meditation. As we rest our mind in God, we are not only guided, we are renewed.

The effects of prayer and meditation are cumulative. The more we practice, the more spiritual power we accumulate and this power ministers to us in our need. It improves us in every way, from refining our perceptions to expanding our capacity to love and be loved.

These five principles are our partners in creating an intimate relationship with God, one that is truly, powerfully cocreative. The principles are life changing only as they are applied in every area of life. It's great to know how to play tennis or dance the samba, but the knowledge is meaningless unless we apply it. It's great to know how to balance our checkbook, but the information is useless unless we actually do keep it balanced. The miracles come when we apply these five principles in our daily lives.

We will be working with these principles throughout the book. As you begin to weave these ideas into your approach to prayer, you will find that you begin to see life not as a problem to be solved but as an adventure to be lived wholeheartedly. You begin to build the kind of mental clarity that sees beyond obstacles to the great potential and possibilities in your life, and in so doing you will become a valued support to others as well.

Beginning a Prayer Practice

1. To begin, I invite you to try this simple affirmation:

> *Affirmation: With God at my side, I take life in stride and my day is blessed with good.*

2. Start your day with a little prayer. Ask God to guide you in making good decisions, to help you accomplish all that you need to do, to help you be loving and wise.

3. At the end of the day, say thanks for any and all good things that happened.

As the days pass, watch to see how you feel and notice the timbre of your days. Are you experiencing more peace? Are the days smoother?

Prayers

Here are a few prayers to get you started, followed by relevant affirmations. The prayers come from my own needs and yearnings and have helped me out of my own darkness.

It is helpful to memorize affirmations so that they are at your fingertips when you need to replace a negative train of thought.

Loving Lord, I come to You today asking that You open the way for a deepening of my trust in You. I give You my worries, my burdens, and fears, confident that You will make something useful of them. I give You all my hopes and dreams. Thank You for showing what to do to make them come true.

Affirmation: With God all things are possible and nothing is impossible.

Affirmation: God's love in me helps me love wisely, honestly, and generously.

Lord, God of love, let me walk in the rhythm of Your love and wisdom. Tap out Your rhythm in my heart that I might make beautiful music in the world with my life. Thank You for conducting my life today. I expect miracles.

> *Affirmation: God's music in me balances and harmonizes my day in wondrous ways.*

God of love, give me a passion for the life You have given me and for the tasks You have put in my hands. Give me a passion for the important things, the beautiful things, the meaningful things. I thank You for making these the rhythm of my joy and my peace.

> *Affirmation: I am fulfilled, joyful, and passionate in my work. God is my partner.*

God, awaken me to see myself and others through Your eyes. Shine Your light and dispel the shadows. Help me to be vitally alive by being graciously authentic with everybody in my life.

> *Affirmation: God's love helps me love and accept myself and others. I am free to be the best me and to see the best in others.*

Chapter 2

How Should I Pray?

*For I know the plans I have for you, says the Lord, plans
for welfare and not evil, to give you a future and a hope.
Then you will call on me and come and pray to
me and I will hear you.*
—JEREMIAH 29:12

*As we come into the presence of God with prayer, holding
the prayer steadily in mind and consciously unifying our
mind with the mind of God, we are aware of the
soundlessness of God's word as it weaves itself in and out
through the whole soul and body consciousness,
illumining, redeeming and restoring us.*
—CHARLES FILLMORE

Lord, let my heart be aligned with Your love today. Enliven and encourage me throughout the day. Give me the courage to say what needs to be said. Give me the faith to take action on my hopes and dreams. Bless me and let me be a blessing.

I was visiting with my friend Marguerite in Gainesville, Florida. It was a sultry August afternoon and the sun shot rays of light through the canopy of live oaks lining her driveway as we walked. She had not been feeling well and was concerned about the doctor's reports. I asked if she had prayed. She said no. You have to know Marguerite to know what a shock this was.

She has been praying with others and for others for years. I asked why she hadn't prayed for her own health, and she said, "I don't feel right praying for myself." I began to press her then about how she could come to believe something like that. Finally she said, "Sharon, I don't know how to pray. I really don't."

That is what I hear more than anything else about prayer: *I don't know how.* But here was Marguerite saying this. Those who know her consider her a healer, and even she doubted that she knew *how* to pray. Her comment made me realize that what we don't know is how to pray *for ourselves.* We don't *really* trust God to answer our prayers. I realized that the question we should be asking is, What do I need to know about prayer and God so that I can make prayer work for me?

I have asked that question often myself, especially when I have prayed the best I know how and my prayers still don't seem to be answered. I begin to question myself—am I praying for the wrong thing? Am I praying against God's will for me or am I mis-understanding God's will for me? Am I doing something wrong?

We question the God of our understanding and our relationship with this God. Do I really matter to God? Can I trust God? These are productive and rewarding questions if we pursue an answer, for if we pursue the answer we are drawn into taking action to prove that we can trust God, that we do matter and that we are not doing anything wrong.

The truth is that there are as many ways to pray as there are people. And none of them is wrong. There are no right and wrong ways to pray. Yet there are ways that are more effective than others because of what they accomplish, not only in the person praying but also in the kind of relationship that is developed with God. It is the difference between having an acquaintance and having an intimate, trusted friend that you can count on to be there for you always.

The Power of Yes

The word affirmation has become popular these days as a positive, quick-fix remedy, but I use the word a little differently. The key distinction is intention and consciousness. An affirmation becomes a prayer when your intention is to partner with God in an act of creation and when your consciousness is focused on the power of God working in and through you. As you think, speak, or write your affirmation, you invoke the miracle-working power of God by your intention. Try creating a simple affirmative statement to replace the reason you have for not praying, calling the power of God into it by your intention. Every time a reason not to pray comes to mind, let it go and put your mind on an affirmation that inspires you to pray. An example: I take time to pray and am given time for everything else.

In Scripture, Paul writes about how all of us groan from the depths of our being to become all we can be; that there is a knowing in each of us that there is so much more to us than we have imagined. He says that as we reach out to God in the birthing process, "Spirit helps us in our weakness. For we do not know how to pray, but the Spirit Itself makes intercession for us . . . and we know that all things work together for good to those who love God. . . ."

And so, just as we did in becoming adept at anything, we begin where we are and grow in skill. First the rudiments, then the expansion, then the refinements, then finally every bone in our body is trained.

Before you start praying, it's important to figure out why you *don't* pray. It helps to write down your answers. Then, consider what the opposite would be. If, for example, you say you don't have enough time to pray, change that to an affirmation: I have plenty of time to pray.

In fact, most people who tell me that they don't pray say it's because they don't have the time, they're "too busy" or "so busy I don't even think about it." My friend Judy and I were talking about having a prayer practice, and she said, "I just get so busy in the morning that I feel like I'm running as soon as I get out of bed. But you know, Mark [her husband] prays every morning and every night—on his knees." I told her I was really impressed with that. She said, "I am too. I have never done that. I say night prayers but never on my knees. I know I should pray more, and maybe even get on my knees." Two days later I saw her and she told me she'd tried it. She prayed on her knees in the morning and said that it felt strange but really good.

Now, remember Marguerite? She didn't pray for her own health because she learned somewhere along the way that it was selfish to pray for herself. The thought of being selfish if she prayed for herself was enough to make her think that she didn't know *how* to pray for herself, something she did with ease and grace for others.

Lots of people I've worked with don't pray because they think they have to be perfect in it, that they have to have just the right words. Not true. God doesn't care what words we use; in fact

God doesn't need your words at all. Your words are for you. God already knows what's best for you. God knows the depth and height and breadth of you.

Sometimes we don't pray because we think we won't like the answer that God will put in our hearts, or perhaps we trust God with some areas of our lives and not others. (Try to notice if this is true for you, because the areas you don't trust are usually where your deepest fears are.) My friend Jan didn't pray for help finding a new job because she was afraid God would send her off on some quest to find a new vocation and she wouldn't be able to pay the bills. She didn't trust God's will for her or her own heart. In fact, she was trusting a God of decrease rather than a God of increase.

The Power of Kneeling in Prayer

There is a power in kneeling to pray. It is not easily described and is better experienced. When I pray on my knees, I *feel an inexpressible sense of belonging to the Divine that I don't sense when I am standing in prayer or sitting in prayer. I feel more power in my prayers when I am on my knees. Kneeling in prayer seems to create an automatic response of willingness and trust, a kind of outward expression of an in-* *ward attitude of trust and willingness, and this receptivity is all that Spirit needs to minister to us in every needed way. There is something about being on our knees that releases us from the pressure of having to know the answer and be in control. I have gotten on my knees to pray in the most unlikely places—in my office or in the ladies' room—to ask for God's help. Holy people across faith traditions have been known to pray on their knees. Try it and see if it helps you.*

"I love You, God." Notice how you feel. And remember to listen in your heart for a response.

🌿 *Affirmation: I love You, God.*

2. *Be sure to listen.*

It's well and good to ask for God's help through prayer, but you have to give God a chance to respond. I remember my friend Tom once asking me what my sermon was going to be about that week. When I told him that the title was "The Power of Silence," he asked, "What's that?" I replied, "Silence is a part of prayer. We have to practice being silent so we can hear God's voice." He looked skeptical. "But I never actually hear anything when I pray." I've heard many people say that. I've said it myself. For many, it takes practice to just be comfortable with silence. I explained that it takes practice but that it's in the listening that we learn what God wants for us. Some "feel" God's guidance. Others perceive God's guidance in pictures, "seeing" God's guidance. Listening for God is really about being prepared and expectant.

Sometimes I start the conversation with God by asking, "What do You want me to know and do, God?" Then I breathe and listen. It is like tuning a radio. We move the dial of our mind through the static, always moving closer to the broadcasting station, the still, small voice of God. Trust that God will communicate with you in a way that *you* can understand.

🌾 *Affirmation: I pray with trust and God answers.*

3. *Pray honestly.*

Be willing to look and see what is really so for you. Be honest about your feelings, no matter how upsetting. Talk it all over with God. God is love and does not judge us or make us wrong for our feelings. We do that. God receives all of our thoughts and feelings as the ocean receives rain or as a mother receives the cry of her hungry or hurt child. God as love is a chalice in which all that is unlike it is transformed. God receives all of our feelings, from rage to shame, from intolerance to insecurity, with the face of love that accepts and responds in love, not in kind.

When we dig deep, allowing our feelings to surface, or when we come present to our surface emotions and pray them, we are cleansed. Then we are ready to receive what God has to give. Driving home alone late one evening, I was feeling so lonely and alone. It had been another very difficult twelve-hour day at work and I was feeling abandoned by everybody, including God. Tears began to well up and then pour from my eyes. Spontaneously I found myself screaming—at God. I really let God have it, with a little trepidation at first, and then full force. When there were no more screams left, the silence in me and all around me was a vibrant peace.

Calling the presence and power of God into all our feelings and circumstances in prayer begins the healing, freeing process. When we pray, the Spirit of God graciously meets us where we are, healing what needs to be healed and revealing what needs to be revealed.

> *Affirmation: I give my worries to God and God blesses me with peace.*

4. Come to believe that God is big enough to handle everything in your life.

My friend Char told me that after the attack on the World Trade Center she could not pray. She could not reconcile the God of her understanding with such a tragic event. She was having a crisis in faith. She said, "That event impacted me big-time spiritually. I had a hard time accepting that there could be a loving God who would let this happen."

She continued to talk about what turned it around for her. "Then someone sent me an e-mail called 'Where was God on September 11?'" As Char said, "I was shown that God was in all the love that was shown and that God was in the thousands of people who helped. After that I was able to pray and just started acting as if I trusted God again."

Pray your way to a God that is big enough to handle everything in your life, knowing that every crisis in faith is an opportunity to know God better, to know of the infinite power and resources of God.

Little by little Char came to reconcile that event in her heart through *praying anyway*. She prayed for understanding, and in the process the God of her understanding grew larger—big enough to be seen in the event and through the event.

Think about an impossible dream that you hold in your heart, whether it has lived there quietly or boisterously. Think of the most difficult thing in your life right now—a broken relationship, loneliness, an unfulfilling job that you feel trapped in, a difficult person. Is your God big enough to encompass and resolve this? Begin to pray from a mind-set that God *is* and see what happens.

I recently ran into an old friend, Brenda. Her weight had fluctuated dramatically for years. She had tried every diet in the book. She'd go down a size or two but before long was back to where she started, overweight and unhappy. When I saw her this time, she looked the best and thinnest I had ever seen her. I told her so, and asked, "How did you do it?" She was all smiles. "I had a spiritual awakening around eating. I finally got it that it wasn't going to happen automatically, that I needed to ask for help."

Brenda went on, "I didn't think God was big enough to release me from overeating. Then I got in touch with the fact that I really didn't want to quit overeating. I wanted the freedom to eat what I wanted. I told God that I was willing to be willing to quit overeating. I became willing to do what I had not been willing to do before—have an eating plan and count calories. When I did that I became conscious, and in that discipline, my desire to overeat was lifted. Then I realized that I had actually been a prisoner of eating. Now I am no longer a slave to eating. It's great!"

In the same way, we can be prisoners to our own thoughts while thinking we are really free. We tell ourselves we can't have the job of our dreams, the kind of relationships we long for, the fun and creative expression we hunger for. If we will pray for help, be willing to embrace a bigger God, a God with whom all things are possible, we may find, as Brenda did, that there is a whole new world of joy and freedom on the other side of those prayers.

If we will pray from the faith that God's help and guidance lives in the midst of all of circumstances, and be willing, as Brenda was, to change our attitude and perception, we find that God is far bigger than the problem and is, in fact, the solution. Because of her beliefs about what God would and wouldn't, could and couldn't, do, Brenda's God wasn't big enough to help her overcome her eating disorder. When she became willing to extend the boundaries of her beliefs, a new world of possibility opened. Through praying from this new perception, she not only saw her situation with new eyes, she was also given the power to do what had previously seemed insurmountable.

When we face a situation that challenges our faith, God is, as Scripture says, standing at the door of our life knocking. If we will open the door of our mind, God will minister to us in ways that guide us to overcome the challenge and grow our faith. God is bigger than all of our difficulties and each difficulty brings us to the threshold of knowing this. Praying with a willingness to know this helps us across the threshold.

Be sure your God is big enough to handle all the challenges in your life. If not, embrace the kind of God who is. Then simply begin to act as if it were true.

> *Affirmation: With God all things are possible, including this.*

5. *Release your problem to God.*

Some years ago, I worked as a sales consultant for Mary Kay Cosmetics. When I first started I was terrified. I knew this job would put my greatest fears right in my face. It could mean rejection. I had to ask people to buy something from me and I had to face feeling rejected if they said no. I was so afraid that I found myself praying all the time. I prayed for the courage to make the six cold calls a day that we were told was a key to success; I prayed before doing a beauty show in a stranger's home and before working the room to make my sales.

Little by little, my confidence grew, my fears diminished, and my business flourished. Through prayer I was given everything I needed. The fear didn't go away *before* I made the calls or did the show. No. Through prayer I was given the strength to make the calls and then the fear went away. And that new freedom from fear spilled over into every area of my life.

It is in releasing the problem from our mind and heart and into the mind and heart of God that we find peace. And given that the effects of prayer are cumulative, and that the more we pray the happier we become and the better life gets, the "best" way to pray is to develop a dedicated, committed practice.

> *Affirmation: I let go and know that God knows what to do and is doing it.*

6. *Pray with the understanding that thoughts are things.*

This was one of the most astonishing and life-changing things I heard in ministerial school. Thoughts are things—they have life, substance, and intelligence. They actually occupy space in our consciousness and in our bodies and have intelligent life that will cause them to develop and grow—to be fruitful and multiply. This phenomenon underlies the third basic principle introduced in Chapter 1—thoughts that we hold in our mind produce after their kind, or, what we think about we bring about.

Bonnie has struggled with allergies for most of her life, each year fearing their onset and hating their presence. She would start dreading allergy season long before it arrived. The season would arrive full-blown. She had prepared well for it by building a set of thoughts and emotions that supported the problem.

She told me that she had recently been reading about the power of being present to our thoughts and our capacity to stand back and observe thoughts without resisting or fighting them. She decided to try an experiment. Every time her allergies flared up, instead of thinking how she hated the symptoms, she would observe them with compassion. She said, "When I just stop and observe them, I shine light on them. I ask God to heal them and reveal anything I need to know. They are actually dissipating." We can deconstruct unhelpful beliefs in this way, one thought at a time.

Barry noticed how he was beginning to feel restless and discontented with his work as a conflict-management consultant. He was dissatisfied with the process being used and its results. People on both sides of the conflict seemed to end up feeling victimized. He prayed for guidance in finding a process that would be truly healing, that would create peace. The more he thought about the possibility the more passionate he became. He began to talk to experts in the field, read books, go to trainings. In time a vision of how things could work came to him. He wrote a proposal that was accepted by his organization and he was on his way to fulfilling a dream.

He said, "God gave me a vision that I could make a difference in creating world peace. At first I rejected it, thinking that I could never do such a thing. It was way too big for me, but little by little, every time I work with a group, teaching the principles of peacemaking, I see that that vision is possible. I keep asking myself and inviting the people I work with to ask themselves: 'How can I be the way of God in this conversation, in this circumstance?' "

With our thoughts we construct our lives. Every thought is a building block that eventually builds the home of our life.

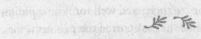

Affirmation: I think good and good happens.

Create an International Environment for Prayer

Creating a place for prayer that *feels* sacred enhances our sense of connection to God. It also powerfully develops our relationship to God, self, and all of life. The internal *and* external environments are important here and one impacts the other. Scripture urges us to take great care of our inner environment. The biblical Book of Proverbs cautions, "Guard your heart with all vigilance; for from it flow the springs of life."

What if you were to bring the sacred into every room in your home as well as your work space as a reminder of your connection to God and of the sacredness of all of life? What if you surrounded yourself with things that are sacred to you, that remind you of a power greater than yourself? Imagine it. Everywhere you turn you are reminded of God. I have had my home and office rearranged using feng shui (the ancient Chinese science of optimally balancing and harmonizing one's environment in order to enjoy great good fortune), locating the areas of wisdom and putting sacred objects and pictures, like an altar, in those places. Try it. If you've never done this, keep an open mind and start small.

You can create an altar anywhere—a small table, a bookshelf, even a box. Put something personal on the altar as a symbol of making your intentional connection with God—maybe a photo, a memento, something collected from a favorite place, a gift from someone special. Maybe include other special things like candles, favorite pictures, flowers, statues of angels. You can bring symbols of the Divine and the sacred anywhere, blessing yourself and your environment. Your world becomes a living prayer.

I put small chimes in my car, hung from my rearview mirror. Their sound makes me feel as though angels are riding along with me. I have friends who put favorite short prayers and affirmations on the dashboards and visors of their cars. Others I know put affirmations on their refrigerators or desks, or inside cabinet doors.

It is helpful to plan a regular time of the day to pray. Try enfolding your day in the energy of prayer by starting and ending the day in prayer. This helps to create an internal environment of prayer. Your prayer in the morning fills the cup of the day with nourishment. Closing your day in prayer fills the cup of your night with blessing energy. Just as regular physical exercise builds and maintains the health and vitality of the body, so regular prayer builds and maintains the health and vitality of your spirit, soul, mind, and heart. And that in turn nourishes the vitality and well-being of the body.

Another step in creating an intentional environment for prayer is to search out a prayer book or two that soothes and inspires you. I use a monthly booklet of prayer thoughts called *The Daily Word*, along with my *Twenty-four Hours a Day* prayer book. I supplement those with various prayer books that I have found in bookstores, sometimes only reading a page at a time. I keep *The Daily Word* on my desk as well, and in the midst of a hectic day, I'll pause and read the page for the day again and feel refreshed.

Make creating a beautiful and inspiring environment for prayer an exciting project for yourself, an environment that invites you to prayer. Try lighting candles. I do it with intention and awareness, reminding myself that the light of the candle is a symbol of the presence of God in me and all around me. I use scented candles because I like feeding all of my senses with beauty. I also burn my favorite incense. Experiment with the things that most give you a sense of the sacred.

Allow time for reflection. What ideas and guidance have come to you during your prayer time? Try journaling your thoughts, keeping track of your prayer life and the development of your relationship with God through a journal. Some inspiring books have been written about the power of journaling. I buy a new journal at the beginning of the year and start by writing down my dreams and goals for the year. The rest of the pages are filled with my morning conversations with God. I write down questions, pause, and pray, asking for God's will and guidance, and then write what comes to me.

My friend Rita has created an amazing prayer journal. She cuts out prayers that have inspired her and pastes them on the covers. When she finds a new one, she creates a page in the journal for it and adds her own thoughts. She finds pictures or creates her own in response to the message of the prayer. Each day as she writes she includes her feelings, her dreams and desires, her stresses and struggles—she gets it all out on paper. She told me, "This is one of the best things I've done for myself. It's a work of love for me, and I love looking back and seeing how God has worked in my life."

All of these intentional practices help to create a mind of peace, and it has been rightly said that it is a mind of peace that precedes all healing. When our thoughts and emotions are chaotic, we can't perceive the guidance of the still, small voice of God above the racket in our inner environment. Breathing deep, long breaths affirming that you are breathing in the light, the life, and the love of

God is a wonderful way to calm the inner turbulence. Breathe deep and let go of any disturbing thoughts or emotions. Breathe into them with compassion and then let them go into God. Affirming that your breath is the light, life, and love of God, breathe it into every cell and atom of your being. You might try breathing in an affirmation like "I now breathe in the peace of God." As you exhale, breathe out the difficulties, stresses, or tensions.

Jesus said, "Peace I leave with you. My peace I give you; not as the world gives do I give to you. Let not your hearts be troubled. Neither let them be afraid." He continued to reassure his disciples, saying, "In the world you will have tribulation; but be of good cheer. I have overcome the world." He was promising that while life is full of challenges to our peace of mind, there is something in us and always available to us that is far greater than all of it. It is the peace of God that passes all understanding. And it is only a thought and a breath away.

What you are creating with these simple practices is an inner and outer environment that raises your vibration and the quality of your thinking, and in and of themselves the practices can transform our emotions. These simple things ready us for receiving the gifts, graces, and guidance of God. And as we practice, life gets better and better.

Affirmation: In my sacred space, I am guided and graced.

One afternoon I went to our shipping department to send a package off to my grandsons. Karen was there to help me and as she got me the forms to fill out, I asked about the pictures on her desk. As she pointed to the picture of her daughter, who had just given birth to Karen's third grandchild, Karen's eyes welled up with tears. She told me that the baby girl was born with a heart defect and they didn't know if she'd make it. We prayed right there in the midst of boxes and scales.

On a tour of the Holy Land, a group of us had gathered in the ruins of the king's palace at Jericho and spontaneously formed a circle to say a prayer that the trip be safe and blessed. It was both.

Above and beyond everything, *how* you pray is not nearly as important as that you *do* pray. Anytime, anyplace, anyway can work. Just the act of reaching out in some way to a power greater than yourself engages that power to bless you in some way, if it is only to calm your quivering heart for a moment.

Beginning a Prayer Practice

1. Pick one or two of these suggestions to focus on this week, paying attention to how you feel in the process and how your day goes.

2. Create a prayer room in your home, experimenting until you have a space that most nourishes you in your prayer practice.

Prayers of Devotion: Aligning with the Divine

Lord, God, flood my heart with the grace of Your presence. Let me feel the peace of Your assurance, confident that a miracle awaits me today. I am ready and I claim it now. Thank You, God.

God of infinite wisdom, I open my whole being to be penetrated by You now. May all my thinking reside in the beauty of this oneness. May all my choices rise and all my actions spring from it.

Dear God, pour in me today as all of the resources I need. Kindle the kind of courage in my heart that overcomes my fears. Deepen my faith, expand my capacity to love, and broaden my horizons for what is possible in my life.

God of life and author of my fondest dreams, I open myself now to Your pulsating presence. I am willing that You inhabit my thoughts and guide my steps throughout the day. I am excited to experience the fullness of You at home in me.

God of wonders and miracles, I embrace Your steadfast love, imagining it enfolding and suffusing me now. I cling to Your brilliant presence that guides me ever into a renewal of hope and a resurgence of the power that sets me free to become all You would have me be.

Chapter 3

Aligning with Divine Mind:

The Power of Focus

The Gulf Stream will flow through a straw,
provided the straw is aligned with the Gulf Stream
and not at cross purposes with it.
—ANNE LAMOTT, *Bird by Bird*

Let what you say be simply yes or no. . . .
—MATTHEW 5:37

Most amazing God, whose breathtaking power parted the sea of troubles for the Israelites and whose magnanimous generosity fed their hungry souls in the desert, come now and swallow up my doubts and fears, my stresses and struggles, in Your unfathomable love. I cast my burdens to You now in trust that You will deliver me into freedom.

My first grandson was a strapping ten-pound baby who was born with a set of lungs that could command a battalion. Once he learned to walk, his very favorite thing to do was to go outside for "walks," which were more like runs. He would bound down the sidewalk until something caught his attention, like a sewer cover, or a flower, or a front door. He would make a cursory investigation, then turn quickly and move on to some other fascinating attraction. Everything he laid his eyes on was alluring.

My role in all this was to corral him. When he insisted on going into every open garage and tinkering with whatever he could find, like lawn mowers, shovels, tires, I'd pick him up and turn his focus to something harmless, if only for a moment. I'd carry him over to a flower bed and invite him to touch the flowers as I named them. He'd invariably rip one off its unyielding stem, and I'd be hoping that the owner of the home wasn't watching as I responded, "No, no, Blakie, pretty flowers, smell." He was never much interested in just smelling.

Our minds tend to be like that—toddlers running in every direction, sometimes incredibly creative and sometimes running oblivious into dangerous terrain. Our great discipline is to corral these always-busy minds of ours and lead them away from contaminated waters of fear, blame, jealousy, self-deprecation, resentment, harsh judgment, or envy, and toward the refreshing waters of constructive thoughts. That's what prayer does; it aligns our thinking with infinite wisdom and love.

Prayer is not about focusing our creative energy on God for the purpose of changing God or motivating God to get moving on our requests. It is not about focusing our energy to turn God around to our way of thinking or doing. It is about disciplining the tendency of our mind to run off in many directions, thereby dissipating our power, heading us, often enough, down blind alleys and potholed paths. Prayer is about focusing our creative capacities, which are infinite, on God so that God's presence can be apprehended and embraced and welcomed to minister to and through us.

As you continue to answer the call to adventures in prayer, you will experience God transcendent and God immanent—God everywhere present outside yourself, working with you through the people and circumstances of your life, and God at the center of your own being, guiding, healing, strengthening, and comforting you. While you may believe that God is present everywhere in the universe, prayer opens the door of your awareness to actually experience the activity of God, the grace of God. You will recognize God working through the people and circumstances of your life in ways that you could never have plotted on your own or even imagined. You will hear someone say just what you needed to hear at just the right moment and appreciate that this is the grace of God. You will notice the immanent activity of God as changes in yourself—changed attitudes, perceptions, and character qualities.

The story of Job in Scripture tells of his spiritual awakening to the presence of God. As he considered the sudden downward turn in his "luck," he began to feel abandoned by God. With the challenges to his faith so severe, with his losses and pain so great, with feeling so powerless in the midst of it all, his faith was slipping through his fingers. He turned inward on himself, hating himself and wishing he were dead. It is a classic example of faith grappling with adversity, one that we all experience.

The story ends with Job meeting God, not on his own terms but on God's terms. Job sees God with new eyes. As we pray in the midst of all that life brings, we too come to see God and our relationship with God with new eyes.

The courage you are not sure you have; the beauty of your deepest, purest dreams and desires; the spark of love that grows into compassion, kindness, tolerance; the ounce of strength that grows into courage, patience, perseverance; the kernel of hope that grows into enthusiasm and passion that bring joy and life to all you do; the persistent yearning for peace and harmony with all people and all of life; the growing urge that leads to doing the right thing; the creative energy that shows up as your gifts and talents and uniqueness—all of this and more is the life of God within you. Theologians call it grace. All spiritual traditions have a name for the dynamic activity of God in us.

In this chapter we consider the importance of focusing your mind through prayer, because the more you do so, the more you will see God active in your life. Being able to focus in prayer also allows you to apply the power of prayer to all the major arenas of life, including making good choices and wise decisions, creating harmonious relationships, handling change and difficulties, and experiencing expansive abundance and ineffable joy. (Each of these is the subject of a later chapter.)

Thomas Merton, the Trappist monk and mystic, who authored close to a dozen books on spirituality, beautifully describes the purpose of focused prayer. He says, "We come to know God by seeming to touch God. It is a response to a call from the God Who has no voice and yet Who speaks in everything that is, and Who most of all speaks in the depths of our own Being."

Jesus Christ said, "You are the light of the world. A city set on a hill cannot be hidden. Nor do they light a lamp and put it under a bushel basket, but rather on a lamp stand and it gives light to all who are in the house. In the same way let your light shine before all so that they may see the good that you do and give glory to God." When people see our light shine even in the midst of difficulties and stresses, they recognize a goodness, a power that is greater than our humanity, and they can't help but be touched. When your light shines, it awakens others to their own light.

Jesus was not the only one to point to the light of God being within us waiting to be discovered and uncovered. Leaders from traditions across the spectrum of spirituality talk about ways to uncover the light of the Divine within each human being. It is the light that created and pervades the universe and each of us.

Focusing your thinking through prayer is like taking the bushel basket off the light of God in you. It not only lights your way, it lights your thinking with clarity. The energy of your prayer little by little dissolves the darkness of the protective shell you have built around your tender, vulnerable heart, the darkness that can distort perceptions, block the flow of love, misdirect your decisions, and toxify your body.

As you focus your mind on aligning with divine mind in prayer your energy clears and becomes lighter. You become like incandescent light because you become energetically purer. You become a presence of peace and joy that brings light into our world. Your prayers can then become like laser beams, so focused, so coherent, that nothing can stop them—or you.

A Few Simple Focusing Steps

There are some simple steps that can help tame the toddler in our mind and focus the awesome power of our thought in prayer.

Start with several deep breaths and lift your thoughts Godward. Paul suggests in his letter to the Philippians that we can turn our thoughts Godward by thinking about whatever is noble, just, pure, lovely; whatever things are of good news; any virtue and anything praiseworthy. Any loving, kind, appreciative, grateful thought begins to focus your creative energy Godward. You don't even have to *feel* like thinking of these things. If you will just do it anyway, you'll get there and harvest the benefits.

Try it. Think about someone you appreciate. Write them a

short note and tell them. Try praising someone. See how you feel and notice the clarity that comes to your thinking. When I am out for a run on a clear, crisp day, I focus on the beauty all around. I focus on my favorite color combination—the deep green pine trees framed against a cerulean blue sky. I silently say thanks to God for the amazing beauty spun out before me, and my spirits are lifted.

Now, begin to rein in your mind and give it instructions. The mind loves to wander in the fields of past memories, seeing if they can be adapted to the present and future. More often than not the mind will wander in fearful and hurt fields, which tend to look like fields of flowers rather than the weeds that they are. Begin to take your mind off any problems and focus on a spiritual truth: with God all things are possible; God is love and so am I; God is light and so am I; God is power and so am I.

Finally, bring the full power of your focus to the intention to be a channel, or straw, if you like Anne Lamott's metaphor, through which the presence of God can move with ease, ministering to you in any needed way.

As thoughts come, let them pass as the scenery passes when you drive down a road. Keep your focus on the road and enjoy the ride.

One of the ways I focus my mind, reining it in from all the compelling excursions it wants to take, is to imagine light filling my body. I "watch" it enter at the top of my head and, like the current of a river, flow through my entire body.

Like silently walking through a pine forest bathed in the scent and the noonday sun above, you are being nourished by God beyond words.

Then you can speak your prayer into this energy and sense in a way that you can understand the response of the One.

In my first pottery class, the teacher, a master potter, began with a simple rule. He said, "Be careful of the speed of your wheel. If it goes too slowly you will not be able to form the bowl. If you get the wheel going too fast, the clay will go off-center and collapse." Focusing our thoughts in prayer is getting the wheel of our creative mind to turn at the perfect speed to let the Master Potter create an exquisite bowl of our lives, our hopes and dreams and deepest heart's desires as well as our difficulties. Our thinking and feeling don't go off-center nearly as much then.

I recently took my three grandsons on an adventure to Science City in Kansas City. One of the hands-on attractions is a high-wire ride on a bike suspended about twenty feet off the floor. There is a net beneath the wire and a 250-pound brick balance fastened beneath the bike. I dared 8-year-old Blake, the eldest of the three boys, to try it. He said, wisely, "After you, Gramma." So, of course, up I went. As the nice lady strapped me in, she gave me a pep talk of reassurance. She promised there was no way I could fall because of the weight balance. She said, "Just keep your eyes on me and you'll be fine." Terrified, I began pedaling backward with my eyes locked on her as the bike eased across the wire. I stopped halfway and pedaled back, feeling exhilarated—and grateful.

The same practice of locking our mind on God when life gets scary eases us across the chasm of the unknown and back home to safety.

Denial and Affirmation

In Chapter 1 we looked briefly at the idea that denial and affirmation allow us to take dominion of our thoughts. They are the two complementary tools we have to help us transform our consciousness through prayer. Denial and affirmation are the spiritual tools that focus our thinking with intention and precision. In this way the whole quality of our thinking improves. We take charge of the quality of our thoughts rather than letting them take charge of us. Through the use of denial and affirmation we take our mind off the problem and put it on the realm of true solutions, the mystery of divine grace.

Two-year-olds know all about denial. "No!" is often their very first word, and they know how to use it with lightning accuracy when confronted with something they don't want or don't like. In the same way, through prayer we can use the power of denial, our no-saying power, to withdraw attention from something negative or unhelpful. A self-destructive thought, emotion, belief, attitude, or perception can simply be denied the energy of our attention, which keeps them alive and active even beyond our awareness.

We all know that the more we think negatively or let our thinking linger on a problem, the worse we feel. This will never get us where we want to go. The key is to catch ourselves in the negative train of thinking. When we do, it is useful to say a prayer like: "I deny the power of this person to upset me." Or, "I release this fear of being rejected."

The denial is a form of prayer because we are invoking a power greater than our personality to release us from the negative condition or perception. We take the control away from the condition or perception, speaking from the power in us that is greater than the condition. We don't deny the fact. We deny its power to drive our thinking and behavior. We stop investing our creative energy in thinking that only robs us of joy and peace of mind. Instead we shift our investments out of issues that deplete our resources and capacity for enjoyment and into thinking that pays rich, life-enhancing dividends.

The next step is to quickly fill the void created by the denial with an affirmative prayer, an affirmation of what we want to experience: "Thank you, God, for the loving people in my life." Affirmations invoke the power of the Divine abiding at the core of our being to do in and through us what our personality cannot now do. We are binding to our experience a heavenly truth, having asked the divine Alchemist to transform what we do not want to experience. This spiritual prayer practice of denial and affirmation has been described in Scripture as a consuming fire. The dross is consumed in the fire of divine love, and the delicious essence of goodness remains.

Bonnie was in a relationship that had become difficult and painful for her. Yet she wanted more than anything for it to work out. Her partner had become distant and sullen with her career successes. He would be very close and supportive one minute and then suddenly become aloof and back off. She said to me, "I just don't know what to do. I can't live with him and I can't live without him. He is so unhappy with his life, and his depression is bringing me down. He just can't be there for me."

I prayed with her using a denial and affirmation: "Bonnie, I know that God has a positive plan for this relationship and that it is safe for you to let go of all worry and fear of loss. Let go of all thought of Paul's depression and changeableness into the healing love of God, knowing that God goes before you this day making straight your way into peace and confidence. We release your relationship to God now in faith and affirm that the activity of God is doing what needs to be done to create clarity and peace in your relationship with Paul."

Denial erases, dissolves, and releases. Affirmation claims, plants, and builds.

Denial withholds energy from a thing. Without energy nothing, including a lifelong belief, can live. Through denial we erase from our consciousness not only self-limiting, untrue beliefs, painful emotions, and longtime resentments but also the compulsion toward self-destructive habits. Once these self-limiting beliefs are released, affirmations, which are the seeds of all that we deeply desire in our lives, find fertile soil in which to grow.

A Changed Destiny

The young Myrtle Page had been sickly most of her life and in her twenties was hospitalized for a year with tuberculosis, a disease that had taken many in her family. At thirty-five she married Charles Fillmore and in a short time they had three sons. However, her health continued to decline, as did her hope. The turning point came in 1886 when she was given only six months to live. She and Charles went on a spiritual search that led them to a lecture that was the catalyst for changing her life and, ultimately, her husband's. She was told that she did not inherit illness, a statement that utterly defied the family belief system.

She chose to believe this radical new idea and set about educating every cell and atom of her being to it. She wrote to a friend, "I had been laboring under the belief in inherited ill health (and)...I awakened to the Truth that God is my Father and that I inherit from Him only that which is Good." She began a daily, dedicated prayer practice, using denials and affirmations as the foundation. She would deny the power of the illness and her belief that illness is inherited. Then she would affirm radiant life and energy pulsing through every part of her body.

Myrtle Fillmore kept her focus on the good she desired. She was healed. The tuberculosis disappeared and she went on to live some fifty vigorous and creative years. As a result of her "miraculous" healing, friends and neighbors came to her for prayer instruction. Her husband, Charles, began to experiment with the same practices and experienced his own extraordinary healing. Together, they went on to found Silent Unity, the Unity School of Christianity, and become leaders in a spiritual renaissance.

You, too, can experience extraordinary results by focusing the power of prayer in this way. You, too, can change your destiny.

After years of wishing Paul was different and doing her best to change him, Bonnie came to believe she was powerless to make him over into her image and likeness of a partner. She also came to accept her own needs in a relationship. They separated for a year, each willing to release the other in love. Each was committed to their own spiritual growth, and I can't speak for Paul, but I know that Bonnie diligently practiced releasing her need to have Paul be her way. She had to release her hold on the relationship as well, having at some level believed that her happiness depended on it. She affirmed the validity of her needs as well as her dreams and desires. As she focused her energy on taking action on what she did want, doors opened for her and her dreams did begin to come true.

A year after they had separated, Bonnie and Paul found each other again and decided to try building their relationship on a new foundation, gradually.

Today they are still together and are happier than ever.

How to Use Denial and Affirmation in Prayer

Denials and affirmations become more powerful the more we use them. I like to write them, read them, *and* speak them. I often repeat them while I'm working out. Each morning I write them in my journal. Then I look back at what I've written and take in the power of the words through my eyes. In this way they are woven into the fabric of my being and are more likely to accomplish their purposes.

A denial can be as simple as saying no to a negative thought, but remember it is important to immediately refocus your thinking on something positive. Sometimes rather than saying a simple no to a thought that you don't want, you might start talking to God, using a form of denial and affirmation: "Lord, I give these fears to You. Take them and do something useful with them. I don't know what to do with them, but I know that You do."

Then really let go of that train of thought and take charge of your thinking, creating thoughts that bless and encourage you.

Here are three affirmations that I have been saying for the past five years with amazing results:

My entire being is balanced, vital,
healthy, loving, and happy.

My capacity to give and receive love increases
dramatically. I radiate love and magnetize love.

I am fulfilled, joyful, and passionate in my work.
(This one got me out of a depleting situation and
into a job about which I am truly passionate.)

The most effective practice is to pair a denial with an affirmation and use them together. Here is a set that a friend gave me. I have them written on a piece of paper that I keep in a prayer book I use each morning. I see them and speak them each morning in prayer and again during the day whenever I think of it.

Denial: I now release all people, places, and
situations that are not a part of the divine plan for my
life. All people, places, and situations that are not a
part of the divine plan for my life now release me.

Affirmation: I now attract all people, places, and
situations that are a part of the divine plan for my life.
All people, places, and situations that are a part of the
divine plan for my life now attract me.

Here are some other pairs:

There is nothing to fear, for the power of God in me is
greater than my fear. I release this fear to God (denial)

>   *and give thanks for the power to take*
>   *right action* (affirmation).

>   *I let go of all resentful thoughts about* _____ (denial)
>   *and wish him/her all the good things*
>   *I wish for myself* (affirmation).

>   *I let go of all worry about money* (denial) *and know that*
>   *the abundance of God is manifesting in wondrous and*
>   *beautiful ways in my life now* (affirmation).

Experiment and find what works best for you. Create paired sets of denials and affirmations that fit your particular circumstances. You might even say a prayer, asking God to guide you in creating sets that truly excite your heart and feel soothing to your mind.

You might be asking yourself, "What if I don't believe what I am saying?"—like wishing good things for someone who has really hurt you. I know I did. Maybe it feels impossible or even threatening. The good news is that all that Spirit asks of us is our willingness. Sometimes I have had to pray for just the willingness to be willing. It has always come. With our willingness the great Alchemist has an opening to work with us and do for us what we cannot seem to do for ourselves.

In those moments, remind yourself that releasing resentments and fears of any kind are for your own freedom and happiness. Your freedom from fear and resentment is the highest and best contribution you can make to creating peace on earth. When you free yourself, odd as it may seem, you free others. What we do for ourselves spiritually is a contribution to the whole world.

⚹ ⚹

Should We Pray Generally
or Specifically?

People often ask me whether they should pray for specific things or just pray "Thy will be done" or something general like that. The answer is, there is a time and place for both. Paradoxically, perhaps, both general and specific prayers get their power from our ability to focus.

We often pray specifically—for things we don't think we can manifest on our own. In reality, this is how we prove God to ourselves and grow our faith to the point where we can move the mountains in our lives and create heaven in the earth of our experiences. I keep a button on my desk that reads "P.U.S.H." It stands for "pray until something happens."

There is a story about Mr. Jones, who dies and goes to heaven. He is met by St. Peter, who tells him that he will now be given the heavenly tour. Amid the splendor of golden streets, beautiful mansions, and choirs of angels, Mr. Jones notices an odd-looking building over to the left. He asks St. Peter to see it. St. Peter tells him that he really does not want to see what is in there. This, of course, piques Mr. Jones's curiosity, and now he won't rest until St. Peter shows him what is in that building. St. Peter finally relents. It turns out that the enormous building is filled with row after row of shelves, each stacked nicely with beautiful white satin boxes tied with big red ribbons.

St. Peter says, "These boxes all have names on them, Mr. Jones."

Mr. Jones asks, "Do I have one?" to which St. Peter replies, "Yes, you do, but frankly, if I were you I wouldn't . . ."

No stopping Mr. Jones, who dashes to the *J* row and finds his name. Pulling the ribbon off, he opens the box, looks inside, and lets out a soulful groan, one that Peter has heard many times before. There in Mr. Jones's white box are all the blessings that God wanted to give him—except that he never asked.

That's the specific part.

When should we pray generally? How do we know when to "let go and let God," when to say, "Not my will but Thine be done"? It is a matter of monitoring the texture and emotional state of your thoughts and your prayers. Ask yourself: Am I now attached to the outcome, trying to force a solution in my prayers? Am I becoming impatient and insistent that divine timing match up with mine? Am I beginning to feel hopeless, worried, anxious, or even angry that what I have been praying for is not happening? If so, it is time to relax and let go. Begin to pray in generalities—Thy will, not mine; this, or something better.

When we let go and let God, we let go of being in control and knowing what the next steps and outcomes will be. I call this praying dangerously because it defies our humanness, which needs to feel safe, protected, and in control at all costs, minimizing the unknown in every way. Yet, in this dangerous—or adventurous—kind of prayer, we come to know a God we can trust. As we let go and wait for God, we come to know a peace that passes all understanding. We wait for clarity. We wait for guidance for right next steps. We also wait for God by giving our best, being our best, and seeing the best.

As I see it, general prayers are "dangerous" in three ways:

First, they are prayers of surrender. When the disciples asked Jesus, "Lord, teach us to pray," the prayer he gave them, the prayer still said countless times throughout the world every day and at eleven o'clock every day at Unity, opens with surrender. We say,

> Our Father Who art in heaven, hallowed be Thy name. Thy kingdom come, Thy will be done on earth as it is in heaven. Give us this day our daily bread. . . .

In the opening sentence we acknowledge our relationship to one another and our intimate relationship to a power greater than ourselves. In that understanding we surrender into that power that is heaven, utter goodness, inviting it to manifest on the earth of our daily experience. And, rather than tell God how we want this goodness to show up in our lives, we surrender our personal will and ask for God's will. We yield in humility, desiring that the goodness that God is make its home in all the moments of the day. We go even further in trust when we ask for our daily bread. We are asking for God to give us what God thinks we need. We trust that God knows better than we do what we need.

Second, general prayers are "dangerous" to our humanness because they are prayers of acceptance and willingness to change, and be changed. We hear this in the Serenity Prayer:

> God, grant me the serenity to accept the things I cannot change, the courage to change the things I can, and the wisdom to know the difference.

The prayer asks for help in accepting life on life's terms. It asks us to let go of trying to change people and circumstances to get them to be as we would like.

In it we ask for the courage to change the only thing we can—ourselves. It may mean we have to leave an unrewarding job or an abusive relationship. It may mean that we give up a cherished belief. It is a prayer of release in which we stop fighting what is. We let go of our insistence on having life on our terms and open ourselves to having life on God's terms.

Third, general prayers are "dangerous" in that we become willing to be used by God, willing to go against our own human proclivities in order to grow the Divine in us. Rather than using God to get what we want, we ask God to use us to get what God wants. As we release our will, we open ourselves to the divine seed in us to grow into the full stature of its potential. We relegate our personality to second position and put our divine character in first place.

The best example I know of this kind of general prayer is the Prayer of St. Francis:

> Lord, make me an instrument of Your peace. Where there is hatred, let me sow love; where there is injury, pardon; where there is doubt, faith; where there is despair, hope; where there is sadness, joy; where there is darkness, light. O divine Master, grant that I may not so much seek to be consoled as to console; to be understood as to understand; to be loved as to love. For it is in giving that we receive. It is in pardoning that we are pardoned. It is in dying that we are born to eternal life.

In this prayer we surrender our whole being, asking to be molded and shaped by God, to be made a straw aligned perfectly with the Gulf Stream of God's goodness in its infinite forms and expressions. As we become instruments in the Master's hand, we die to our humanness and are born into ever-greater expressions of our divine nature.

When you pray in this way, surrendering, accepting, and asking to be used, get ready. God will do things in and through you that are far greater than you can even imagine right now.

Prayers of surrender open the way to a sense of peace. When we feel a sense of peace, having released our attachment to our desires, it is a good time to return to specific prayers. Praying from a place of peace, having released the struggle to get what we want, opens the way to praying with conviction. Conviction is the kind of faith that Jesus spoke of in his healing miracles. When a miraculous healing took place, he would say, "Your faith has made you well."

Not long ago I received an angry e-mail message from an

estranged friend that enumerated my mistakes, reframed history in her favor and my complete disfavor, and discounted my reaching out to heal our relationship. I could feel my insides knot and twist as I read it.

With every bone in my body I wanted revenge. I immediately began to write a response that would match her veiled venom and raise her one. When I finished I took a deep breath before I hit the Send button. Did I really want to send this? I took another deep breath and prayed for help. Every time I thought about it over the next twenty-four hours I would call on grace for help. I prayed, "God, help me see this rightly." It was hard work because all I wanted to do was retaliate for the hurt and anger I felt. By the next morning, I felt some peace. I reread her note and didn't get the same enormous knot in my stomach. I began to see it just the tiniest bit differently. I didn't need to send the retaliatory note anymore. Instead, I was able to write and send an e-mail acknowledging her desire to, as she put it, take care of herself by ending the relationship. I was even able to wish her well and, because I hadn't retaliated, release the friendship with peace in my heart. I could never have done that without prayer and a willingness to do it differently.

So sometimes focus is about letting go of certain perceptions, thoughts, and emotions and letting the grace of God, which is a mystery but entirely real, transform them. Letting go creates a space for grace, a space that is quiet and peaceful. In this space clarity and right direction are revealed. This is a gift of praying generally.

Finally, focus in prayer keeps us conscious and present to our lives. When we pause to pray, we become present to what is so for us. As we focus our thinking Godward, we behold our relationship to our life, to ourselves, and to others. We hold it up to the light of Spirit. There is no greater feeling of vitality, aliveness, and authenticity than this.

Practices for Focusing Your Prayers

1. **In your morning prayer time,** begin by focusing your whole being Godward. Close your eyes, take some deep, long breaths, and let a beautiful word, phrase, or vision come to mind, maybe a word like *love* or *hope*. Maybe using a phrase feels better to you, like "Here I am, Lord." Whatever it is, enjoy it for a few moments, breathing it into your whole body.

2. **Create a denial and affirmation** for a situation that is especially difficult. Write them in your journal each morning. Say them through the day when you're in the shower, driving, feeling restless, or just taking a quiet break in your day.

> There is no limit to what prayer can be: a lifeline in adversity; a steadfast, clear, unflickering light in deepest dark; an out-of-sight companion whom the soul loves well; refreshment from a hidden spring, a field of flowers, a hermit's cell; for every need a gift of grace; in quietness and confidence a yielding into Love's embrace.
>
> —What Prayer Can Be, R. H. Grenville

Focusing Prayers

Dear Lord, in my hurried life and demanding days, help me to remember that You have given me each day to live fully and creatively alive, each day crossing some threshold into a fuller expression of Your life in me.

Dear God, I open my heart and soul to experience Your presence. Let me have my mind so aligned with You that I feel an ineffable peace and joy. Let me know as Jesus Christ did the intimacy of Your presence abiding at the center of my being.

God of love and freedom, of second chances and fresh starts, move across the waters of my heart, warming it with faith that births courageous action. Touch me with the truth that sets me free to take chances, build bridges, mend fences, and love lavishly, knowing that You stand at the door of my life today calling me into the good that awaits me.

God of infinite wisdom and power, help me focus my mind in You. Everything goes better when I do. It's so easy for me to forget, to be so distracted that I don't even think to turn to You. Keep reminding me today that You not only have what I want, You are what I want.

Loving Lord, shine Your Light into all the nooks and crannies of my being. Show me what I must release so that I can be truly free, be the loving person that I want to be, and draw to me all the great possibilities You make available to me.

Dear God, grasp me now and keep my mind focused on You, letting me feel the incredible exhilaration of Your guiding care and protection.

Part Two

Focusing the Power

In Part One, I talked about prayer as the vehicle for connecting with God—accessing the power, passion, and purpose of God for our lives. Just as in order to make a home appliance work, we need to plug it into the electrical current in the wiring, in order to access the power of God, we need to pray. In order to open ourselves to the potential of God in us and all around us, we focus our thoughts on God through prayer.

But it takes more than just realizing the need to pray. Your prayers become most effective when you train your mind to tap into the great creative source that is God in a focused way. Author and scientist Gregg Braden calls it "living in the mind of God." Learning how to direct your thoughts in prayer with clarity and precision opens you to receive the infinite resources of God that you need and desire.

Chapter 4

Healing the Heart:

Prayers for True Relationship

This is what I ache for: intimacy with myself, others and the world, intimacy that touches the sacred in all that is life. This ache, this longing is the thread that guides me back through the labyrinth of compromises I have made, back to my soul's desires.
—ORIAH MOUNTAIN DREAMER

Dear God, I open my heart to the fullness of Your love, grateful that it opens the way to true intimacy with You, myself, and others, grateful that what needs to be healed is healed. Amen.

In all of the counseling and praying I have done with people, I've never met anyone who didn't struggle with relationships. Accepting people just the way they are without trying to make them over into our image of a true friend, lover, partner, sibling, or co-worker is too difficult for our humanness. The same is true of our own relationship with ourselves. This is why we have to ask for God's help.

There is nothing like a relationship to set all your good beliefs about yourself askew. There is nothing like a relationship to lock you out of all your well-decorated rooms of sanity and safety.

At the same time, in all the counseling and praying I've done with people, I've never met anyone who didn't want to create vibrant, supportive, healthy relationships. Our hearts hunger for robust, nourishing relationships, for the presence of another who draws out the best in us, who allows us to be safely authentic.

Our relationships are truly the threshing floor for the development of the Spirit of God in each of us. It is here that a door opens for us to see who we really are, what we are made of. It is here that we discover how the presence of God in us strengthens and expands our capacity to love.

On the threshing floor of relationship, we get to separate daily the wheat of love from the chaff of self-centered fears in all their disguises. When we crack the protective husk built by fear, the most delicious, nourishing, and fortifying food of life is released. A gentle vulnerability emerges. The heart and mind hunger for such nourishment.

If you don't have love in your life, no matter what else there is, it's not enough. Yet loving everyone all the time is impossible for us human beings. We need the power of Spirit, the activity of God, to overcome our automatic judgments and tendency to relate based on what separates us rather than what joins us. It takes a power greater than our humanness to overcome the pain of betrayal, the fear of loss, the need to defend, and knee-jerk justifications.

Great spiritual masters, teachers, and leaders of all faiths have attributed their extraordinary capacities to the Divine. Jesus said, "I of myself can do nothing." He knew that his extraordinary capacities, including his capacity to love his enemies, came from the power of God at work in and through him.

And so in this chapter we bring relationship to the forefront of our adventures in prayer. We become willing, hopefully, to be a little more courageous in all of our relationships through the power of prayer, ready to venture into the mystery of making our invisible desires visible.

Seven Practices for Healing Relationships and Increasing Your Capacity to Love

Following you will find seven spiritual principles and practices for healing relationships so that they become vibrant and healthy, so that they will nourish the soul as well as mend the heart. Whatever relationship concerns you most as you read today—a new marriage or a troubled one, a conflict between parent and child or a conflict at work, a lost friendship or a draining one, a difficult coworker or demanding supervisor— you will find a prayer practice that will help you.

1. *Take God as your partner in all relationships.*

First, take a look at your relationship with God and make sure you are not afraid of God in any way. When we have a trusting relationship with God, we have a model for all of our other relationships. Trusting God allows us to truly trust ourselves and others.

If you still have ambivalent feelings or distrust or anger toward God, ask yourself what it would take to change those feelings to ones of trust. What would it take for you to feel that God is your partner? Work on finding a God you *can* love and trust with everything, at all times. Try to ground your prayers in the most positive, powerful, inspiring, comforting concept of God that you can imagine.

Growing up, Laura was surrounded by constant threats at home and church of being punished by God. Early on she turned her back on God, shunning a relationship that she believed would hurt her rather than help her. When she was a teen, she found another god in alcohol. Finding a strength and courage that she desperately needed, alcohol became her best friend, a constant companion.

When her world came crashing down and the courts ordered her into a recovery program, she was told that she needed to find a higher power she could trust and that prayer was the way. "I hated the idea. I didn't even want to hear the word 'God,' let alone pray my way into a relationship with God, but I wanted my life to get better. I started by just saying, 'If You're there, please help me.' I began to notice that I was feeling better, that things in my life were going better. My husband and I were getting along better and I wasn't getting angry all the time with people at work."

Start with simple prayers: "God, help me handle my relationship with (fill in the blank) in a loving way today," or "God, what do You want me to say to this person right now?" "God, what would help right now to know and do?"

Now breathe deeply and rest yourself in an alert listening. God, it is said, speaks softly in the silence of your listening. So we have to turn down the internal racket and be fully present in an expectant kind of silence to hear God's response.

Sometimes God guides us to do things that go against old, ingrained patterns and so we want to discount or dismiss His advice. That is why practicing with little things helps.

Ed was working with a team on a project for his management class. He found himself regularly getting angry with one person on the team. "She's bossy and always thinks she has the best ideas for our project," he said. He began to pray for patience and understanding. Toward the end of the semester, things had changed. He said, "She's really pretty nice. She brings me little treats every week now." A little thing that changes everything.

When I can remember, I just ask God, "Who can I love for You today?" Names and ideas always come. Little thing, little risk, big dividends.

Sometimes just asking for what we need and want in a relationship is difficult. In our fear we often express our desire in a way that is hard for the other person to hear, blaming them for what they are not doing rather than asking for what we want. Instead take a moment and ask God to speak through you. Start with a small request like: "Will you drive to the theater this time?" "I don't feel like cooking. Can we go to dinner tonight?"

Ask for guidance, then act on what comes to you. It may be scary at first, but do it anyway. Keep expanding and increasing the scope of your asking for guidance, asking in bigger ways and for things that are most at risk—a marriage, a relationship with a family member, a friend, or coworker, a job. With practice the screen of your heart will become clearer and clearer and your inner hearing finer and finer.

Affirmation: God guides me in all of my relationships, giving me the words to say and the actions to take. I go to God for help and I receive it.

2. *Develop a trusting, intimate relationship with yourself through prayer.*

As we grow a more trusting, intimate relationship with God we find that our trust in ourselves grows as well. Because we come to understand that by turning to God in the difficulties and disappointments, the misunderstandings and misgivings, and asking for help and courage, we set free the Divine in us that is more than strong enough, wise enough, loving enough for anything we face.

I remember a friend calling in tears one day. She was feeling terribly guilty and out of control with her anger. She said, "I find myself yelling all the time. I argue with Steve constantly and today I was screaming so loud at Tommy for leaving his toys outside that he started crying. I'm afraid of my anger." I told her that God would help her with this if she would ask. I said, "Pray each morning for help through the day. When you feel the churning inside and the anger coming on, pause and breathe and ask God for help with what to say."

The next time we talked she told me how she had started praying during the day while at home with the children. She said, "I pay attention now and when I feel the anger coming on, I stop myself and go sit alone, if only for a moment, and pray. I just ask God for help, and it's working."

When you develop a consistent prayer practice, the alchemy of prayer takes the ore of your humanness and turns it into the gold of your spiritual nature. The veil of your consciousness is pulled back to reveal a "you" that is exquisitely beautiful, astonishingly powerful, amazingly strong, competent, and wise, and totally lovable—the image and likeness of God individualized as you.

For some people a frontier is just asking for what they need from their spouse. Saying "I need more time together" or "I need some alone time" can feel threatening to some who haven't yet learned to trust the validity of their needs. For some a daunting frontier is handling conflict in a relationship effectively. The automatic fight-or-flight response is the only one they know. In fact handling conflict effectively is a worldwide relationship issue. The flower children of the '60s and early '70s had a motto regarding the Vietnam War: "Make love, not war." Some have not learned the competencies that prevent war—whether in the home, school, neighborhood, workplace, or the world.

Many of us grew up with poor examples for resolving conflict in our homes, schools, and even churches. We never gained competency because we were not taught how to embrace our fears or how to embrace conflict and use both as a way to grow the Divine in us. Perhaps we don't know how to disagree effectively, how to leave a relationship without blame, how to be loving without "enabling."

Trust in God and ourselves grows in the soil of courageous action. I like to pray simple audible prayers at the frontiers I face: "Okay, God, give me the words to say." "Dear God, take my fear and do something useful with it. Help me say what needs to be said." "God, guide me here." "God, I am going to do what I think You are guiding me to do. If I've misunderstood, please stop me."

Carter and Alec had been best friends for three years, in the same class and inseparable on the playground. Now in third grade they found themselves in different classes. Carter was heartbroken. His mother, who is my daughter Jennifer, was concerned because for the first time he didn't seem to like school. One day early in the school year, Jennifer was called to come pick Carter up because he was sick. On the way home she asked him if something had happened at school to upset him. At first he denied that anything had happened, but then told her that Alec wouldn't play with him, that he had a new best friend and that at lunchtime Alec had made fun of Carter's new shoes.

Seeing Carter hurt so deeply, the protective instinct in Jennifer was fired and she decided to call Alec's mother. She was so angry, she said, that she was as afraid to make the call as Carter was to tell her about his hurt. "I prayed that God would help me talk about it without blame," she said. "I said that Carter was actually sick because he thinks Alec doesn't like him. I asked if Carter had done something to Alec." Alec's mother wanted to help the boys resolve the conflict too. She said that she would talk to Alec. It wasn't long before Alec called Carter to apologize, saying, "I didn't mean I hated your shoes, Carter. I was talking about the girl next to you. And I thought you didn't want to play with me." Jennifer, at a frontier of competency with anger, prayed and was given the words that led to resolution. Alec and Carter were able to cross a frontier of competency about resolving conflict as well.

It is through putting ourselves on the line over and over again, feeling the fear and doing it anyway, that we become all we are meant to be.

> *Affirmation: God in me is greater than any relationship difficulty I face and helps me resolve it.*

3. Take dominion of your thoughts.

The headline on a flyer I recently received about a conference on spirituality read, "Life is short and immense. This precious opportunity asks of us that our time here be purposeful, joyful, and a blessing to others." How do you and I make our days here purposeful, joyful, and a blessing to others? By making a choice each day about what we will honor by our thoughts, by deciding to see the cup of our day and our relationships as half-full, not half-empty.

Suzanne came to see me because she was having a very bad

day. She recounted to me the people who were annoying her and why, her disappointment and disillusionment with her employers, and the irritation she felt with the man in her life. I asked her to consider what she was honoring and what she wanted to honor. I asked, "Do you want to see the cup of your life today as half-full or half-empty?"

I asked Suzanne to pray for each of the people who were upsetting her peace of mind. By asking her to pray for them I was asking her to take dominion of her thoughts. This, you will recall from Chapter 1, is the fourth basic principle: denying the negative and affirming the positive.

Taking dominion of our thoughts is one of the most demanding yet powerful spiritual practices for creating healthy relationships. When we try to use our personal willpower alone, the work is strenuous, tedious, and usually has mixed results. When we take charge through prayer, however, we build spiritual muscle, which makes it possible to continuously expand our capacities.

I remember being stunned the day I heard and understood for the first time that I had a choice about what I thought. It was a new and immediately empowering idea.

I began to notice how often I would take things personally, how often my negative thoughts would run away with me. Slowly, I learned to stop, pray, and choose again.

Cynthia was startled by a late-night call from her son, a bright and promising junior in college. He had been jailed for drunk driving and needed to be bailed out. After blistering Derek with how irresponsible he was, she told him that he'd have to call her father—his grandfather—and explain it to him. That was the worst kind of punishment, since Cynthia's father and Derek adored each other. As I listened to her story, Cynthia constructed a scenario of devastation: this incident was just the beginning, Derek was going down the tubes; he would fail in school, not graduate, wind up in some shop fixing bicycles, or worse. The situation had definitely taken dominion of her thoughts and was straining her relationship with her son and her husband as well, who seemed able to remain calm and objective about it all.

Lisa can't be in the same room with her mother without intense negative emotions. Her emotional state is pretty much dictated by her mother's behavior. She had become hostage to her negative feelings about her mother.

She called me in something like panic when her mother invited her and her two young children over for Thanksgiving dinner. This infuriated Lisa, convinced as she was that it could only be a distasteful and disasterous experience. "I don't want to go. What should I say?" she asked. "I want to tell her that we're going to be out of town. Actually, I don't even want to talk to her." She gave me chapter and verse about how intolerable her mother was. After listening for a while I offered that if her mother could do better she would, suggesting that Lisa pray before calling her mother. She called me later to say, "You know, I really feel good. I was able to listen to her trying to make me feel guilty for not coming for dinner and not react. I told her that the kids and I would stop by for a little while. I think it will be okay." Pausing to pray breaks the cycle of allowing people and circumstances to determine the quality of our thoughts and emotions.

Initially, the work of taking dominion of your thoughts is tedious. Our responses to any sense of threat in a relationship are so well-practiced that they are automatic. It takes great presence and persistence in prayer to change the patterns. It is normal to want to give up, but don't. Let your spiritual muscles feel the stretch and know that they are growing in power.

I remember one day feeling utterly exhausted with this business of noticing my negative thoughts and reactions. I was weary of the spiritual work of paying attention, catching myself taking things personally, letting the thoughts go and replacing the negative with something positive. I found it far more demanding than the workouts my trainer would put me through at the gym. I screamed out to God, "Please help me. I can't do this." A kind of compassion that I couldn't even name at the time flooded my heart. The sense of burden was lifted and little by little the automatic negative thinking and reacting diminished. Becoming the guardian of my thoughts grew into a work of love after that. It will for you, too.

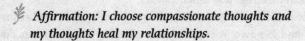

Affirmation: I choose compassionate thoughts and my thoughts heal my relationships.

4. *Practice forgiveness.*

The fourth way of healing a relationship is the practice of forgiveness. Each time there is a challenge in a relationship the automatic human reaction is to fight it or run from it. The Spirit of God in us would have us find a third way—release and freedom through forgiveness.

But how do we forgive? I don't think "we" do. I am not so sure our humanness can. But if we are willing and take certain steps, the dynamic, organic Spirit of God does. As we place our resentments in the chalice of the Divine, a certain alchemy takes place, turning resentments to compassion, not, perhaps, overnight, but with our dedication to the practice, surely.

It may seem difficult and even undesirable to do the spiritual work of forgiveness. Once hurt deeply, no one wants to be hurt in that same way again. There lurks the fear, often disguised as a "just cause," that if we forgive we will be vulnerable to be hurt again—manipulated, used, abused, or betrayed. We might tell ourselves that the person does not deserve to be forgiven, that the deed is unforgivable—like the husband who can't forgive his wife for having an affair; the woman who can't forgive her husband for beating her; the child who can't forgive the parent that deserted the family; the student who can't forgive the teacher that belittled him. Yet in cases where, for example, a husband and wife have been able to forgive each other, both people are set free and love grows. When we are willing to forgive and begin to pray for the person who has hurt us, we are strengthened and fortified so that we can release the person from the grasp of resentment and set ourselves free at the same time. The second gift that comes to us through forgiveness is immunity from being hurt in the same way again.

Susan was the oldest in a family of six children. She was a single parent, having left a man who was physically abusive. When she found out that her father wanted to divorce her mother she was outraged. Her mother was devastated. Her brothers and sisters were shocked and angry. The family was being torn apart and people were taking sides. When Susan found out that her father had been having an affair, she swore that she would never forgive him. She refused to speak to him and excluded him from all of the family holiday celebrations in her home.

That was almost eight years ago. Today Susan and her father have rebuilt their relationship and it is more loving than ever. But it took a long time. At first Susan wasn't even willing to forgive her father. Yet she came to realize that her justified resentment was making her unhappy. She couldn't talk about her father without getting angry. Her road back began with her praying for willingness to forgive him. The willingness came slowly, but it came. As her heart softened, she began to pray for him, just asking God to bless him. One day she found an orchid at her front door. No card, but she knew who it was from. Her dad used to buy orchids for her mother and all the girls in the family every year for Christmas. Susan's heart melted as she felt very special to her dad once again. She was ready to invite him to Christmas dinner at her home and back into her life. Little by little, prayer by prayer, the relationship was healed.

Sometimes in our pain we direct our anger toward God. A young couple loses their baby to crib death; a child is murdered on the school playground; an athlete's career is ruined with the onset of a disease. Such crises bring us to the brink of all we believe about God. The childlike desire to be shielded and protected by God from the harsh realities of life is awakened. Our shocked response is often to blame God for what happened.

Blame in any relationship breaks the bond, and so, just as we would with the people in our life, we restore the bond with God first through forgiveness. For the anger we feel, we give our willingness to know more of God, to deepen our understanding, to see the situation differently, to heal the relationship.

Holding resentments, no matter how justified they may seem, drains our creative capacities, especially our capacity to love. Resentments are like weeds that crowd out the flowers of free-flowing expressions of love. They take up space in our heart that could otherwise be occupied by enlivening, connecting ideas.

A Simple Practice in Forgiveness

Looking over all of your relationships past and present, is there anyone that you feel separated from, anyone you wouldn't want a phone call or visit from or wouldn't think of calling? List their names. Pray, asking God to love them through you. Wish for them all the good things you wish for yourself. Continue the practice until you feel a sense of ease and peace when you think about the person, until, instead of a negative reaction, you feel neutral or even compassionate.

Each time you engage the energy of divine love through the conduit of forgiveness, new doors to your own creative expression open; you are given more volts of spiritual electricity and can operate at higher levels of effectiveness in every part of your life. Every forgiving thought is a powerful healing prayer for yourself as well as others.

Forgiveness is a process, and part of that process, the final step, is making amends. We amend our thinking and our behavior. We becoming willing to change. If we have harmed someone, we go to that person and apologize, asking to be forgiven. At the same time, we make a commitment in our heart not to repeat whatever caused the harm.

There are only two situations when direct apology is inappropriate. The first is when it is premature. Sometimes we just want to get the apology over with so we can feel free again or feel the relief of taking care of unfinished business. If we have not yet dissipated our anger through prayer, an apology won't work. The other is the case when an apology would clearly cause more harm. For example, for a husband or wife to apologize for having an affair out of the blue or in a sensitive moment without a context and preparation, might do more harm to the person betrayed. Sometimes what is most helpful is to repair the harm by amended behavior. This is why prayer is so important. We ask in prayer for pure motive, clarity of intention, and guidance about right action.

If you have been offended, try to see what you might do differently so that you do not walk away again from such a situation with a grudge. Did you omit saying something you should have said? Did you say something you should not have? What expectations or beliefs allowed you to feel offended?

As you continue in the practice of healing resentments through forgiveness, you will notice a lessening of defensiveness, a greater capacity to speak your truth authentically, to ask for what you need and desire, to disagree without being disagreeable, and to embrace conflict as a way to grow. This all creates a heightened sense of aliveness and an exhilarating sense of freedom and peace.

One more thing—the most important person to forgive is *you*.

Affirmation: I give my resentments to God and God gives me the freedom to love.

5. *Learn to accept people as they are.*

We cannot make clear, wise decisions for ourselves until we can accept other people just the way they are and be open to the truth of a situation. But that does not come easily to us. The Serenity Prayer is one of the best prayers I know for reaching out for God's help in accepting what our humanness cannot: "God, grant me the serenity to accept the things I cannot change, the courage to change the things I can, and the wisdom to know the difference." In other words, the only person I can change is myself. Who I am may affect another, but I cannot have any peace in trying to change another.

Similarly, how another is acting may affect me, but I cannot make changing that person the motivation or justification for my behavior. No amount of pleading, placating, punishing, or manipulating can change someone. Accepting a person does not mean that we must accept everything they do, especially when it is hurtful to us. In this case, acceptance may mean coming to terms with the fact that their behavior is not going to change, and that we must keep ourselves out of harm's way. We can only change how we look at it and what we do about it.

In my marriage, for instance, I could not accept my husband's anger. I thought that if I would try harder, just agree with him, not confront him about anything; if I would change one more thing about me, he would not be angry. I resisted his anger, altering my behavior to try to control it. None of it worked. After trying everything I could think of to keep him from getting angry and losing myself in the process, after talking to one therapist and friend after another, I hit a wall. That's when I heard, as if for the first time, what a friend of mind had been saying—if he never changed, could you stay with him? I finally had to accept that I couldn't. It took releasing a lot of guilt to get there, though. I had to admit that maybe other women could live with it, but I could not. With that acceptance a door opened for me.

At that point I was able to leave the marriage and slowly begin to look at my own anger, which I had been resisting and denying forever. I realized that his anger was a mirror of the anger that I had kept hidden in the shadows of my heart. The divine in us never expects or intends us to be victimized or abused.

Sometimes our expectations of both ourselves and others are unreasonable. We expect perfection of ourselves, afraid of making a mistake, thinking that being wrong means *we're* wrong. We feel angry and let down when others fail to measure up to impossible standards. The *Wall Street Journal* once ran a cartoon showing a man and woman sitting knee to knee on a couch. The man is gripping his knees with his hands, looking bewildered. The woman is gesturing with both hands as she says, "You're sensitive, caring, loving and nurturing, but that's just not enough anymore." We can make the mistake of expecting another to meet *all* of our needs, when it is our responsibility to make our own happiness. Or we experience a conflict of needs. One person needs space and another needs intimacy.

My niece Genny was about to be married in Houston, and it was one of those rare opportunities for the family to be together. My daughter Jennifer, who lived in San Diego, was in turmoil about her cousin's wedding. Her husband had a business conference that same weekend, and he wanted Jennifer to come with him. In any case, he did not want to fly to Houston for the wedding. Jennifer's heart was torn.

Though Jennifer was six years older, she and Genny had always had a special bond and could always be found together at family gatherings. Besides Jennifer's big-sister relationship with Genny, our whole family had been close in her growing-up years. Holidays and birthdays were family events. Actually, any excuse was a good one for a family party.

Jennifer's and John's values and priorities were clearly at odds. Who would give in? Or was it a question of giving up? Would either of them be willing to give in, praying for a win-win solution?

We all face these kinds of situations in relationships—times when we have conflicting needs and values. We face this in ourselves as well. We have needs and values that are in conflict. Prayer is the way to find a peaceful resolution.

While she kept hoping John would change his mind, Jennifer told me that she was praying to know what God would have her do. When I called a week before the wedding, she said, "I've been praying, Mom, and I've decided not to go to the wedding. I'd really rather be with John than anyone else and this is a chance for us to be together without the kids. I know it's the right thing." Jennifer had not given in under pressure or fear. She had faced squarely into the conflict, and then asked God's help in her decision. She was truly at peace.

Next time you are in the midst of differing opinions, values, and desires; in the midst of clashing purposes, needs, and perspectives; pause and breathe into the conflict and pray for help to accept what is so for yourself and another. Pray for guidance for the next right step.

You may have seen the question, "What would Jesus do?" on posters, coffee mugs, bracelets, or bookmarks. It's actually a very good question to ask in such situations. If "Jesus" doesn't work for you, you might ask, "What would love do here?" Or think of a spiritual master who is a model for you, and ask what that one would do. Then do it.

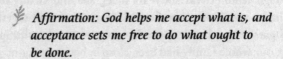

Affirmation: God helps me accept what is, and acceptance sets me free to do what ought to be done.

6. Ask others for spiritual support.

An even more powerful way than praying on our own to invite God into our relationships is asking others to give us spiritual support. Having others hold a high vision for us—either for healing a current relationship or attracting a vibrant new one—not only expands the healing power of prayer but also brings us a heightened sense of confidence and reassurance that something good will happen.

We so often isolate ourselves with our troubles, feeling that we ought to be able to figure everything out on our own. We may be embarrassed and even ashamed to be having trouble or confusion in the first place. It takes courage to reach out for help when we feel vulnerable. Yet asking someone we trust to listen prayerfully and pray with us for understanding dilutes the trouble and lights the darkness of confusion with clarity.

Asking for spiritual support is not about finding a receptive ear for our complaints or being bolstered in being right while making another wrong. It is about helping us see our part, and what we can do to improve the situation.

David and I were consulting one afternoon about a project he was working on for the church. At the end of our discussion, I asked what I could give him. He said, "I'd like about ten minutes of your time to talk about some personal stuff." I suggested we sit down, and he continued, "You know Allison's daughter and granddaughter are living with us now and I am finding that it's affecting our relationship. Allison is so busy with Taylor that she doesn't have time for me. Or she is so exhausted at the end of the day, she goes to bed early and we don't get to connect." He went on, "I am not being who I want to be with Allison's granddaughter either. I brush her off and avoid her. I feel really bad about it."

We talked about his feelings of anger and resentment. He said, "I am afraid to say anything. I don't want to make Allison angry." I told him that he couldn't *make* Allison angry. I went on, "If you don't speak your truth in love, resentments will definitely grow and the walls will get thicker. God will help you say what you need to say from a loving heart if you ask." We prayed and I affirmed, "God is love and wisdom in you and will give you the words to say and the power to say them from a loving heart. Thank you, God, for giving David the right and perfect words to say and the power to speak them from love."

He felt empowered and, as he told me the following week, he did sit down with his wife to share what was so for him. When he spoke he was calm and could speak from love for her and valuing the relationship. He said, "I feel better. She could accept it and I am seeing a shift."

> *Affirmation: I trust that God works through people, and I reach out in trust for help.*

7. Embody the love you desire and give to others what you want to receive.

When we give the best of ourselves to another for God's sake, the best in us not only expands, it comes back to us multiplied. When we give the gifts of appreciation, encouragement, and kindness to others, we engage the infinite resources of God to return those very things multiplied. This is how the universal spiritual law of giving and receiving works.

There is a story of a rabbi who lived alone in the forest. Monks from a nearby monastery would often pass his shelter on their walks through the forest.

Their monastery, once a popular destination for people from all over the world because of its beautiful grounds, welcoming monks, and delicious food, had fallen on hard times. The monks still went about their daily tasks, but the spirit had gone out of what they were doing. There was no joy, no devotion, and little fellowship. Visitors had simply stopped coming.

One day the abbot called the monks together to discuss what to do. It was decided that the abbot would seek the advice of the rabbi. And so he went the very next day and told his story to the rabbi, asking the rabbi what to do. The rabbi commiserated but said that he could not help. They prayed together and read the Torah. The abbot thanked the rabbi, and as he rose to leave, the rabbi stopped him. "Just a minute," the rabbi said. "Before you leave I must tell you this one thing: one of you is the Messiah."

The abbot was stunned. "Thank you," he said, and ran back to the monastery to tell the monks.

The monks began to whisper to themselves and each other. "Who could it be?" As the thought began to work in them, they began to speculate. Surely it is the abbot. He is a man of God, a true leader. Maybe it's Brother John. He's so loving and kind. It couldn't be Brother Elrod, could it? He is so cranky. It couldn't be Brother Phillip either. He is so bossy.

On the off chance that it was one of them, they began to treat each other with extraordinary respect and soon they were finding new joy in their work. They began to serve one another. They actually became grateful for one another.

Visitors returned and gradually the monastery began to thrive again.

And so it is with us. When we give our best to one another, embodying the many expressions of love—kindness, understanding, appreciation, gratitude, tolerance, and generosity—we thrive. The activity of stepping beyond our own neediness to give what we need heals us and builds beautiful relationships.

> *Affirmation: I give what I need and
> I am blessed indeed.*

Practices

- **Tonight when you go to bed,** say a prayer for yourself, asking God to show you all the love that lives in you and to help you express it more fully and courageously.

- **Practice saying "I love You, God"** and notice how it opens your heart to loving yourself and others more.

- **The next time you experience trouble** or confusion in a relationship, reach out to a trusted friend for spiritual support.

- **Think of something** that seems to be missing from your relationships. Something that you want more of. Practice giving that very thing to others.

Prayers for Healing Relationship and Attracting Love

Dear God, I pray today that you help me trust a little bit more and stretch my faith to hold more of You. Help my spirit to be a little bit freer and my love to be a little bit wider and my believing a little bit bigger. Help me to give what I want to receive.

Lord, let Your truth be born anew in my heart today in ways that set me free to stand on higher ground and see myself and my relationships through Your eyes. Give me the strength to assume the best and leave the rest to You. When I can see only closed doors, help me find a way to open them.

Most awesome God, Whose love is deeper than the deepest ocean, more powerful than the force of gravity that holds the galaxies in place, and more expansive than the trillions of stars that light the farthest reaches of the universe, come pour Your love in my heart today that I might love more deeply, reach out to others more freely, bind another's wounds more generously, and rejoice in others' good more often.

Most amazing God, Whose grace infuses my often-bruised and tender heart with the courage to risk myself again and again for love and Whose vibrant life penetrates all fears and reluctance with an extraordinary capacity for heroic action, and Whose profound love offers again and again to dance me into dreams coming true, pour Yourself in me now, that I might experience Your amazing grace and goodness in all of these ways; pour Yourself that I might dare great things for You and for others.

Lord, I thank You for Your promises and presence in my life. I thank You for the many times You've helped to make things right. When relationships break down, when I feel all alone, when I feel unloved and unlovable, You come and bring me home to peace. Give me today all I need to mend fences, take chances for love, be my best and leave the rest to You. Let Your music be my rhythm. Let Your harmony be my song, helping me to become a master of love.

Part Three

Expanding the Power

When I first awakened to the power of prayer, I was praying for survival, a way out of or through a difficulty over which I felt powerless—powerless because my best thinking and efforts were not working.

I was praying to bring light into a dark room in my life or to take away the fear and pain. As my prayer life developed, however, I came to realize that we can pray from a consciousness that is not so much about focusing its power on filling a blank in our lives or removing a barrier as it is on expanding the good.

The truth is, we are not meant to struggle and suffer through this life. We are meant to become all we can be, to embody the divine nature that is the ground of our being. We are called to overcome and live a triumphant life. We are meant to embrace and transform the struggles into blessings. We are meant to become greater, not lesser, in the face of life's challenges.

My experience and observation tell me that it is a gradual process, but with dedication and practice we expand our consciousness into a whole new realm. Here we attune our mind through prayer in such a way that we begin to lead more synchronistic and blessed lives. In this expanded perspective, fears lessen dramatically and our faith grows stronger, opening a doorway to a truly abundant life. We are transformed into possibility thinkers.

Chapter 5

From Confusion to Clarity:

Prayers for Guidance

*God speaks to everyone, all the time, and no one is
beyond the reach of His voice.*
—*Our Prayer,* LOUIS EVELY

*If any of you lacks wisdom, let him ask God who gives to
all generously and without reproach, and it will
be given to him.*
—JAMES 1:5

God be in my head, and in my understanding; God
be in my eyes, and in my looking; God be in my mouth,
and in my speaking; God be in my heart, and in my
thinking; God be in my end and at my departing.
—*Old Sarum Primer*

I was so excited as I boarded the plane for Vail, Colorado, and a week of skiing with friends. I was to fly to Denver and take a van from the airport to the bus station in Vail, where I would be met by a friend who would drive me to our hotel. At least that's what I thought. Everything went like clockwork—on-time departure and arrival, van waiting—until we arrived at the bus station and my friend wasn't there. My mind began to race as I sat, praying that he would show up. Did he forget? Did something happen to him? Is he just running late?

After a half hour I began to feel panicky and wondered if I should get a bus back to the airport and head home. I was afraid and angry at the same time. I hadn't thought to get a phone number and wasn't at all sure I remembered the name of the place we were staying. I prayed, *God, what do I do?* I listened as best I could, given the panic that I felt. Bits and pieces of ideas came to me. I heard, "Go find a phone book and see if you can find a listing that sounds like the place." There it was! I dialed the number quickly, only to find the office closed. By now I was in tears. Should I go there anyway? Even if I got there I had no idea what rooms we had.

As I prayed and listened for God's guidance, I felt urged to get in a cab and try it. My heart was pounding out of my chest as the cabdriver let me out in front of the complex and turned to leave. Suitcases in hand, I followed the signs to the office, hoping to be able to rouse somebody to see if my friend's name was on the roster of guests. I rang the office bell. Nothing but the immense stillness of the night. *God, help me,* I repeated, wondering, *Now what?*

There was the "still, small voice" again. "Get in the elevator and go up to the second floor." As I got out of the elevator and walked around the corner, I experienced a miracle: there was my friend walking toward me. The timing of the whole thing was so precise that, for me, it could only have been the amazing orchestration of God. The fact that my friend had forgotten what time I was coming in became insignificant next to the overwhelming sense of gratitude and amazement I felt.

Life forever invites us to grow our faith in a power greater than ourselves by presenting us with experiences that challenge us beyond our current understanding, beyond our own resources, and beyond our best thinking. Life is always seeking to take us over the edges of our comfort zones. It's the currency of the kingdom of faith in God.

As we face the challenge, we automatically search for answers in what we already know, and find ourselves spinning in our own perceptions and experiences as I did that night in Vail. Prayers for guidance open us to the infinite intelligence of the universe that is wisdom itself. In prayer we access this wisdom, which sourced the universe and all of life, allowing it to guide us.

Praying for guidance focuses our mind in the mind of God, taking us out of the dilemma and into the arena of solutions. We clear our thinking of our own will, our opinions about best outcomes, and make ourselves available to divine wisdom, which is pure love always seeking an increase of good.

In this chapter we consider ways of praying ourselves from confusion to clarity, focusing our thinking like a laser beam, piercing the mind that sustains the universe and holds its immensity in perfect balance. Once you discover that there is no place where God is not, you will find divine guidance accessible at all times in all places under all circumstances.

While many of us feel the greatest need for divine assistance when the decisions we need to make are going to be life-altering, praying for divine guidance guides us into right thinking and right acting no matter how big or small the circumstance. The most difficult thing in the process of being divinely guided is making ourselves fully receptive to it. It takes a willingness to release what we want into the field of divine mind.

How do we recognize divine guidance? My friend Lori said, "When I'm doing God's will things go smoothly. When things don't go well I know it's one of my ideas that I've held on to." The prophet Elijah looked for guidance in storms, fires, and earthquakes, and in the end discovered it as "a still, small voice." One thing is true: God speaks to us in ways we can uniquely understand. The trick—and spiritual practice—is to quiet our internal ruckus enough to catch a glimpse, recognize, hear, or sense God's guidance.

Looking for Clues

When my niece and nephew were quite young, my brother-in-law, Donnie, loved to take them on enchanted mystery tours through their neighborhood. Off they would go with only a flashlight to assist them in their search for "clues." "Clues for what?" I once asked. "Just clues, good omens," he responded.

One evening I asked to tag along. We began our mission in the backyard. As we approached the lines of shrubs and trees that bordered their property, Donnie said confidently, "Look! Over there," and he pointed into the trees surrounding the storage shed. We all fastened our attention in the direction he was pointing as he turned the yellow beam of the flashlight to the ground in front of the shed. "Aha," he said, "a clue!" We were charged with anticipation as we moved in to examine the clue at close range. It was an old shoe. We all agreed that it was an important clue and excitedly moved forward in search of the next.

Seeking divine guidance can be like this. As we pray, unsure and standing in the unknown, we have to be receptive to the clues. What is God trying to tell us in the events of our day, in a particular circumstance, in what someone has said? As we listen, what word comes out of the silence?

Standing in the Unknown

I have a friend who works at Renaissance festivals around the country. He reads palms. Hungry for answers, people queue up for hours for his "guidance." I often hear people talk about "their psychic" or "their astrologer." Standing in the unknown is so unpalatable that we not only seek others to predict for us, we tend to force solutions to make things happen the way we think they should. In this day and age we can't tolerate even minor delays, let alone the ambiguities of the unknown.

Our intellect forever seeks resolution, solution, and the gratification of an outcome. This drive is the nature of the creative process itself. Facing the unknown, we struggle to "figure it out," to discern some parallel with a known experience and thus find a way out of the discomfort. Yet there is a season to each birth. Just as we can't rush the birth of a child, we can't rush the birth of our answer. Sometimes it is instantly available, but sometimes the pieces needed for our answer are not yet in place or fully developed. Sometimes we are only given clues and pointed toward a trail where more clues must be gathered.

Jim's wedding reception was held in a room with floor-to-ceiling windows that provided a breathtaking view of the country club's championship golf course. One of the tees was just below the windows. I was at the windows embracing the view as a foursome prepared to tee off. One of the men stepped up to the tee and ceremoniously placed his ball on it, adjusting it up and down several times. He took a long time studying the terrain, eyeing the distance from tee to cup. He then slowly and steadily got himself in place, adjusting his stance a number of times, painstakingly placing the club behind the ball. It looked like he was ready to swing, when he suddenly backed away from the tee and began studying the shot again. He was discerning the way to make the most effective shot given the distance, the trees on either side of the fairway, the varying slopes of the ground.

It strikes me that golf and discerning God's desires for us have a lot in common. The golfer must become one with his club to execute a good swing. He and his club must become one with the ball to produce the most effective shot. The stance, the angles, and the arcs—it all counts. That is so when we seek divine guidance as well. When we take time to study the terrain of possibilities, the depth of our yearnings, and when we seek to become one with God's will, our decisions are well-directed and satisfying.

A Way to Begin

Here is the basic practice I use for discerning God's will. See if you can adapt it to your own purposes.

First I read from two favorite prayer books as a way of getting my awareness centered spiritually. It's like stretching before exercising. Then I close my eyes and begin to silently speak affirmations. Following the guidelines in Chapter 3, you can easily create your own affirmations, ones that paint a beautiful picture of the landscapes of your life. They should be words and ideas that excite and energize you, that are the most positive expression of a desire for your health and well-being, for your relationships, your career, or your sense of worth and value. For example, for relationships I like to say: "My capacity to give and receive love increases dramatically. I radiate love and magnetize love." For work: "I am fulfilled, joyful, and passionate in my work, traveling often to speak and teach." For body image: "I eat with joy and reverence and come to my perfect body weight."

I say these affirmations three times and then begin breathing deeply, imagining as I do that I am breathing in healing, harmonizing light.

This is not only a way of quieting and focusing my mind for meditation, it is a way of giving daily instruction to my subconscious mind.

At the end of the meditation, I begin a conversation with God in my journal. First, I write a question that begins with: Dear God, what is Your will for____? Or, What do I need to know about____? Or, What do You want me to do about____? If my question is about a troubling relationship, I might ask something like: Dear God, what do you want me to know and do about my relationship with____?

I then write whatever comes to me. Then I act on whatever guidance I receive. Sometimes my guidance is to wait or trust. Yet even this guidance is comforting and reassuring.

Another part of my journaling practice is to write who I am willing to be that day in order to produce results that will make me feel really good about myself. What character qualities am I willing to embody to meet the events of the day successfully, no matter what is on my calendar? What qualities will stretch me?

If I need to have a difficult conversation, I name courage. Or, if I recognize that I am having some trouble expressing a certain quality, like generosity, I write it down. In addition to positively affecting my whole day, this practice seems to make my dialogue with God clearer and more open.

I usually name at least five qualities: presence, clarity, focus, joy, gratitude, generosity, impeccability. I notice trends in the qualities I name as well. They reflect what I am working on at the time.

There was a long period of time when "love" and "courage" headed the list each day. I'd pray to have the courage to say the difficult things I had to say with love; to say what I was afraid to say; to be vulnerable instead of defensive.

Often the journaling is about my feelings. It is helpful to get them out of the dark hiding places in my heart and on paper, admitting them to myself. Once I can admit them to myself, I pray, asking God to take them and do something useful and beautiful with them. The sense of relief is extraordinary as the burden of difficult feelings is lifted.

I have often heard the expression "pray your life." I take this to mean dedicating my day to God and God's will, asking God throughout the day to guide my thinking and to direct my choices. I find that to do this grows my faith as well. It means pausing throughout the day to call God into whatever I am doing. Sometimes my prayer is just, "Help me here."

Meditation for Guidance

Close your eyes and rest. Take a deep, long, full breath in and as you let go of your breath, let go of all of your worries and concerns into the heart of God. Breathe deep, rest easy, and hold the thought that the light of God awaits your call. Enter into the silence with these thoughts: Lord, show me the way You would have me go today. . . . Breathe deep and rest into the silence that abides in the still point in your heart and ponder: What in your life is calling you? What in your life is of value? When all the noise is silent and all the meetings adjourn, the lists laid aside, what still pulls on your soul? In the silence between your heartbeats hides a summons.

Think of what you would like the power of the creative intelligence of the universe to cocreate with you. Think of it as a prayer and phrase it in words that excite your heart and stir your hope. Find ways of your own that speak to your heart. The important thing is to begin.

My friend Tess had been unhappy in her job for some time. She had a conflictual relationship with her boss, but most of all the work was not feeding her soul. Yet the income was paying her bills and the thought of quitting to follow her heart and her dreams was unacceptable.

As David Whyte writes in *The Heart Aroused*: "Ten years ago I turned my face for a moment and it became my life." It looked like Tess was going to do that—again. She was released from the job within months and had to consider once again her direction. Would she follow her heart or the paycheck? We prayed and I gave her an affirmation: "God is guiding me." I suggested she make it her mantra, a word or phrase that she would repeat prayfully throughout her day.

She struggled for months, with her faith strong one day and wavering the next. One day I got an e-mail from her saying, "I'm leaning on your faith as well as my own. God is good. I just worry about paying the bills and wonder why my right and perfect job and I have not connected. I know in my soul that God knows what is best. It's just trying to keep my faith when there is no money for the bills." Yet as she stayed consistent in her prayer, she found a hope that seemed to transform the anxiety and fear to a sense of optimism. Almost one year later, she ran into an old friend at church who just happened to have a job opening that was everything Tess had been hoping for.

Our humanness tends to be frightened of the darkness and goes to any lengths to seek shelter from the unknown. Yet, the Spirit of God stands right there with us, and in praying for guidance, we are blessed with a holy encounter. For God always responds.

Imagine that you are a hollow reed through which divine guidance whispers just the answers you need. Keep reminding yourself in moments of confusion that God has a plan for your life that lives in you and that it is better than you have even imagined. Trust that as you seek God's will, which is always good, you will be guided with a right thought or a right action. Be still.

Ask and listen with every bone in your body. Then move your feet.

In addition to listening for God's guidance deep in your heart, "listen" to the events of your life and to other people. God also speaks through them. Start paying close attention to what the people around you say, to what you read, to the day's happenings. Ask yourself what God is trying to tell you. Keep an expectant yet detached attitude, as if watching a fascinating movie: "I will be rightly guided."

When I was first introduced to these ideas, my prayer life was still somewhat hit-and-miss. I tended to turn to God in prayer only when life wasn't working well. Then I'd get very focused, intentional, and consistent. But when life was going well, I was less in touch with God, less interested in seeking guidance.

Surprise, surprise. My hit-and-miss efforts produced hit-and-miss results. Just as being physically fit requires consistent practice, so does spiritual fitness. The more we pray, the more we become a clear and clean receptor for guidance. As I became more consistent in my practice, beginning each day with prayer and asking God to guide me, I began to notice how much clearer my guidance was.

Today I wouldn't leave my home without praying. I begin each day by asking: "What is Your will for me today?" and then I write what comes to me, put it on my to-do list and do it. This simple practice has changed my life and my days. I enter the day with a kind of spiritual confidence, peace, and positive expectancy. Try it and prove it to yourself.

But How Do I Discern
What Is from God?

So far I have been talking about looking for clues and becoming willing to stand in the unknown. But how do we *know* when we are truly discerning God's will and not simply forcing our own thoughts on a situation?

When my children were twelve and thirteen years old, I was not parenting very effectively. They were not doing well in school and were so actively rebelling at home that I was exhausted and feeling powerless. I was trying to control the household in the face of my husband's heavy drinking and, in the process, had lost all sense of self. I remember the ineptness and frustration I felt regarding even seeking God's will. How would I ever know God's will? How would I be able to distinguish it from my own?

What I discovered is that I first had to believe that God's will for me and my loved ones is always good. I had to get really honest with myself, which was very hard to do because I wanted this marriage to work more than I had ever wanted anything.

At first I could not even open my mind to think that I needed to leave the marriage for everyone's good. Over time and with consistent practice, though, I began to trust God. Little by little I saw my fears, insecurities, and defenses for what they were and asked God to remove them. And then I began to "hear" guidance when I asked for it.

This process of cleaning the "house" of our consciousness of the things that get in the way of recognizing God's will is never complete. The best we can do is moniter our thoughts and feelings daily, turning over to God the self-defeating, negative emotions that come up and asking God to do something useful with them.

We are asking the great Alchemist to transform our self-destructive thinking into self-enhancing thinking that leads to right action. It is a demanding practice but worth every ounce of effort for the ineffable freedom, the peace that passes all understanding, and the capacity for joy that result.

The work is about letting go, one thought at a time. God's will can't come if our will is constantly occupying the space. Something as simple as "Thy will be done" opens the way for God to reveal our next right step.

Golden Keying

This simple spiritual practice always works: The next time you find yourself focused on a dilemma or problem, simply let go of the thought of it and put your mind on God. Just saying the word "God" is enough.

Once you have asked for guidance and let go of listening only for what you want to hear, keep your mind focused on God and off the problem. That is the "golden key." Simple but not easy. Just think of God. Think the word "God" or speak it to yourself.

Remember that God speaks through people and circumstances and that the situation may have many pieces that need to be put in place before an outcome can be realized. So while all the pieces of the puzzle are coming together, keep the golden key in the door of your mind.

Work with a Prayer Partner

Having a prayer partner is one of the most powerful things you can do to build your own faith and contribute to the manifestation of the answers to your prayers.

My friend Neal recently admitted to himself that his heart was no longer in his work. He used to find it challenging and exciting, but now the passion was gone and, pray as he would, he couldn't get it back. We became prayer partners in the midst of this. I committed to holding a positive expectancy for him, knowing that God would guide him safely and surely.

His first step was to accept that he had lost his passion for his work and trust that God was speaking to him in this. As he prayed for clarity—to know what God was trying to tell him—he began to feel guided to leave his job. Was he scared? You bet. Did he let his fear stop him? No. His faith had grown over the years to a place of deep trust that he would be taken care of and guided into his next step by the God of his experience. He took the leap of faith and gave notice that he was leaving.

That was all well and good, but now what? he thought. When we talked, he said, "I have no idea what is coming next. I wish God would show me or tell me. I have given my notice. In three weeks I will be without a job." He prayed and waited for the next right step to become clear.

That is the way our faith deepens and our spiritual power expands. We let our past experience of being guided to right choices inform our current experience. If you can't remember a time when you felt divine Providence guiding you, remember a time when you felt confident about a certain choice or decision. You knew that you knew. When you get that sense of an urge in a certain direction after praying for guidance, head in that direction. Ask God to stop you if you have in any way misunderstood the signals. Then start moving.

Neal started to work on his own as a consultant, knowing that there was something more in store for him. But it was not ready yet. All the pieces of that puzzle were not yet in place. Once a month, he and I prayed together for guidance. I would speak an affirmative prayer for him: "I know that God is leading you to the right and perfect work, work that will make your heart sing. You are magnetic to it and it is magnetic to you. Your path is lighted and your way is made clear. You know what to do and you do it with grace and ease."

It took a year. And then the most wonderful, exciting job offer came along—one that he never even dreamed possible. He was offered a key position with an innovative Web broadcasting group focused on delivering inspirational spiritual messages. It was a ministry that he had never even considered seeking but one that integrated all of his education and work experience.

Working with a Prayer Partner

Here's a simple way to get started.

1. *Choose someone you feel openhearted with, someone that you trust wants the best for you.*

2. *Begin by saying a prayer together. Something simple like "We give thanks that the presence and power of God guides us in our prayer time."*

3. *Speak your prayer request to your partner. ("My prayer request is that God guide me to my right and perfect job." Or as Neal did, "I ask that God show me what my next right step is.")*

4. *Write down your partner's request and have her/him write down yours.*

5. *Agree to pray for each other every day for a week (or until you are ready to check in with each other again). In your prayer time, visualize your partner living in the answer to their prayer and ask them to do the same for you. For example, Neal wanted a job that he could be passionate about and that would allow him to travel and teach. So I began to visualize him happy, smiling, traveling, and speaking to groups of enthusiastic people.*

What to Do When the
Guidance Makes No Sense

Sometimes guidance makes no sense but the urge is so strong that you cannot ignore it. Remember that the message may be just one of the pieces in God's more elaborate plan.

When I was serving a church in Florida, I kept getting guidance that a change was coming. I began to question Spirit—what change?—my job, my house? I noticed that I began to feel restless and discontented. I prayed for more guidance. I waited. My daily journal shows that I prayed for months.

As the first step I was guided to sell my home. I had no idea why. Did this mean I was moving out of state or to another city or just to another home? I had no reason to put it on the market. I waited, thinking I might be misunderstanding God's will. The thought recurred consistently over a month and so I put the house on the market. It sold within two weeks, during the Christmas holiday, and I knew something was cooking.

Closing was set for January and I still had no idea where I was going but I began to look. Suddenly the plan changed and closing was moved to July. Now I was totally baffled. I prayed: "What is this about, God? What do You want me to do?" The guidance was trust.

One day I shared the dilemma with a colleague and she shared a prayer that she had used in a similar situation: "Lord, lead me where You need me." I began to use it like a mantra.

There were many more pieces to this puzzle, including my entering into a contract to purchase another home and then being guided to ask to be released from it. When I looked in my heart to see why, what I found was that I wanted to live closer to my children in San Diego. That was indeed the truth but I had no job offer, not even a prospect, in California.

Much to everyone's amazement the owner very graciously let me out of the contract. I took that as guidance to begin looking in California for a vacant church. But now I needed a place to live. It was June and my home was closing in just two weeks. I began to see if there might be something to rent in the same town-house development.

I just had a hunch there would be something. I started asking everyone who lived there if they knew of anyone looking for a short-term renter. Out of the blue I met a neighbor whose family situation required them to move temporarily. She agreed to rent to me on a month-to-month basis with only thirty days' notice required.

I then went about planning a working vacation to southern California. I made arrangements to speak and do workshops at several churches that were open or would soon be seeking new leadership. I was testing the waters. I knew that if one of the places felt right, that would be my confirmation from Spirit. My part was to take the action to check out my guidance.

About a week before my departure, a colleague in our placement office called to suggest that I consider applying for the position of senior minister at a San Francisco church. I declined, explaining that I had already sent my résumé and they had turned me down. She urged me to try again. I agreed and she called them. Ironically, this time they said they were anxious to meet with me. I knew the moment I saw the church that it was the right place for me. The search committee offered the position to me within days, and I was off to a place where God apparently needed me. This, amazingly, was the very same church that my friend who had given me the mantra had left.

My prayer for guidance had been so simple: "Lead me where you need me." And yet the most extraordinary, intricate series of events began to unfold, far beyond whatever I could have imagined and arranged.

That is often the way it works. As we seek guidance for major changes or significant turning points, there may be many pieces that need to be in place before guidance can be clear.

There is nothing in our lives that is too small or too large for prayers for guidance. Decisions about our relationships, our work, our finances, our next conversation, our vacation, buying a house or selling a car, how to live and how to die, how to handle a divorce, how to handle a loss—everything in our lives is fertile ground for calling on divine assistance, clarity, direction, comfort, and protection.

As we endeavor to discern God's will, we begin by telling ourselves the truth about our feelings even though they may be difficult to accept or even admit. We tell ourselves the truth about our needs and desires even though we may find them equally difficult to admit. Someone might judge us selfish. The truth may mean a change that we don't want to make.

At first I couldn't admit to myself that I was discontented in the ministry I was serving. It might mean leaving and starting over and I definitely did not want to do that. I wanted to create a successful ministry right where I was. What I discovered, though, is that feeling discontented was a signal of a deeper call, God's call to a new field of endeavor.

As we search out the truth for ourselves, it helps to contemplate a spiritual principle or Scripture that applies to our situation. For example, I find great reassurance in the promise given in the book of the prophet Jeremiah, "I know the plans I have for you, says the Lord, plans to prosper you and to give you a future and a hope."

After searching for and accepting what is really true for us, including our feelings, our needs, and our desires, and after finding a spiritual principle or Scripture passage that gives us hope, we pray for a clean heart and clean motive. We hold the situation or our desire up in the light of a spiritual principle or Scripture to see how it fares: Is my request for guidance mixed with fear, resentment, selfishness, insecurity? Would it hurt others? When Solomon was told by God in a dream, "Ask what I shall give you," Solomon responded, ". . . I do not know how to go out or come in. Give thy servant, therefore, an understanding mind to govern thy people, that I may discern between good and evil. . . ." And so we do well to lean not on our own understanding, which can never see the whole picture or read hearts, but to lean on divine understanding, which sees the whole picture and reads the heart.

With this understanding we release our will so completely that we seek God's will, nothing more, nothing less, nothing else. Into this pure state of mind, we place the question of our heart for which we want God's guidance. Then we listen. We listen to our heart. We listen to our life. We listen to others. We listen in trust that guidance will come.

When in Doubt, Test

The best test for the guidance we receive is elegantly simple. Ask, Is it divine? Is it loving, kind, generous, compassionate, peaceable, forgiving, truthful? If it is, you can be confident that it is coming from Spirit.

In Scripture, in the Book of James, we find this test for guidance: "The wisdom from above is first pure, then peaceable, gentle, willing to yield, full of mercy and good fruits, without partiality, and without hypocrisy."

James is speaking about what builds bridges rather than what creates distances; about real honesty and pure motive, about self-interest melted into generosity of heart; about a clarity devoid of mixed emotions, about a peace that passes all understanding. These are sure signs of the presence of God. If what we feel guided to do or say brings a sense of joy or peace, if what we say or do builds bridges and creates good, then we can be confident that God's will is in it.

We can ask, is this idea coming from a peaceful place in me? Is my motive pure? Is my heart gentle, willing to yield, and forgiving? Is my guidance partial to what I want or open to what the other may want? If our guidance can meet those criteria, we can feel confident that it is divine. We can also be confident that it will lead us to peace.

It's been said that joy is the surest sign of the presence of God. So if you follow what brings you joy, you can be confident that you are following God's lead.

Following Through

Divine guidance gingerly invites you to cross the frontiers of what you already know into the unknown. Crossing you find, as poet David Whyte suggests, that "you can feel Lazarus deep inside even the laziest, most deathly afraid part of you, lift up his hands and walk toward the light."

To prove the power, presence, and goodness of God to ourselves, to test our guidance, we must take action—make the difficult decision, leap into the unknown, try something we have never tried before, say something difficult to say, take a stand for a value we cherish.

Following guidance will test and prove our faith, too. Our faith is blind until we've put it to the test through action. It grows deep and strong in the soil of action.

The poet Rilke tells the story of the swan who lumbers and sways when walking on land. With each step it appears as though the swan might keel over. Yet it moves ever in the direction of its true nature—toward the water. Once it steps into the water, it is received graciously and carried effortlessly.

We are each like the swan. On land, on our own, we lumber awkwardly. Yet once we step into the water of divine guidance we are carried effortlessly.

Practices for Seeking and Discerning Guidance

A General Practice:

- Set aside time to meditate in a place that brings you peace. Begin by focusing on your breathing, letting go of thoughts as they come. Use a word or phrase to still your mind as you focus on the in breath and out breath, like God, life, love, joy, peace. Think, perhaps, of a word that fits the nature of the guidance you are seeking—for a relationship, for work/career, health, finances, a habit, attitude, emotion. Breathe deeply and embrace the silence. Imagine that you are filled with the divine energy of love and with each breath expand the energy of love beyond yourself to fill the room where you are.

- Let go of all preconceived notions and ideas about the outcome you want.

- Form the question. What are you seeking divine guidance for?

- Be still then and listen deeply for a response.

- Come out of the silence and write what came to you.

- Read it over. Is there some small action to take? A phone call? A conversation to have? Is there an idea that helps you understand the situation? Is there reassurance? Comfort?

- Remember that Spirit speaks clearly in ways that we as individuals can understand. Spirit keeps it simple.

When an immediate decision is necessary or an immediate response is called for:

- Pause and take a deep breath.

- Go into your heart with all of your mind.

- Ask God for a right thought or right response. I simply ask: God, what is Your will?

- Listen expectantly and then speak or act as guided. I often add something like: This is what I think You are telling me to say or do. If not, stop me. (I always pray this when my understanding of the guidance I receive scares me or when I feel unsure about my interpretation of the guidance I've received. And sometimes I have been redirected. A door has closed or there is an unexpected turn in the "road.")

Or:

- Breathe into your heart and go there with all of your mind.

- Ask simply, "God, guide me." "God, what is Your will?" "God, what do You want me to say?"

- Listen and then act as you have been guided. If the guidance feels uncomfortable or scary, pray for strength and get moving.

A Walk in Nature:

- Take a walk in nature and breathe deeply of the colors you see—the blue of the sky, green of the trees.

- And when you feel clear and ready, say, "Speak, Lord. I am listening. What do You want me to know?"

- Listen with every bone in your body and give thanks for what is given you.

- Trust it. Live from it.

A Listening Practice:
- Listen carefully and prayerfully to people you trust. God speaks through people, and your guidance may be there.

- Start watching the events of your life for guidance. What is God trying to tell you in the midst of what is happening?

Affirmations:
I know what to do and I do it.

God guides my path and lights my way.

Prayers for Guidance

Lord, there are times when I think I can't go on, when stress increases and joy is gone . . . times when love disappoints me and friends aren't there. There are times when I've prayed and no answer seems to come, when I've tried and tried and want to run. Right now, Lord, in faith I come to You. Help me hold fast to the promises You gave. Fill me with trust that Your help is on the way.

Dear God, in these quiet moments I come present to the spectrum of choices that I have today and the one choice that will make all other choices beautiful—to be of service to You and others. I release every choice that would not serve You. I am willing to be Your love in action today. Help me say yes to You through the day.

Dear God, in Whose presence I find joy beyond all measure, in Whose hands I am always safe and sound, in Whose love I discover that I am not alone, that I am joined to all others, help me see with Your vision and follow where You lead.

Dear God, quiet me with Your presence and let me rest my driven thinking and behavior into Your peace. Let all my asking and seeking dissolve into Your wisdom and culminate in right action.

Lord of light shine in my darkness and penetrate my fearful confusion and reveal Your will at the center of my being. Embolden me to act in trust that just the other side of my fear is something far better than I can now imagine.

Prayers for Specific Situations

Health and Vitality:

Dear God, what would You have me know and do to heal my body?

Dear God, what would You have me know and do to be in peak physical shape?

Relationship:

Dear God, I want to heal this relationship. What would You have me know and do?

Dear God, I am confused (hurt, angry, etc.) by my friend's behavior. What do You want me to know and do?

Finances:

Dear God, what would You have me know and do to enjoy financial security?

Dear God, how can I be a good steward of what You have given me? How can I make my dreams come true financially?

Self-Esteem, Confidence, Fulfillment:

Dear God, tell me what Your plan for my life is this year. What is Your will? What goals do You want me to set? What do You want me to be and do to glorify You in my life?

Loving Lord, I come to You today as I am, weary of trying to figure it all out so I won't be afraid anymore. I thirst for Your direction to find a purpose for my life that will satisfy my soul. Reassure me that there is nothing to fear, that You are here and will lead me to all that will quench my thirst and transform my fear to faith.

Don't think for a moment that the divine mind that designed the fragrant gardenia and fall colors and Milky Way has forgotten you. Just listen and then you will know what to do, what you are to stand up for and express this day. Strive to be a healing presence. Purify your motives. Let go of judging others, and put love into action. That would be more than enough.

Chapter 6

From Fear to Faith:

Prayers for Making and Handling Change

*To live a path with heart, a life committed to awakening,
we must care for whatever we encounter, however difficult
or beautiful, and bring to it our heart in a great intimacy.
To discover the capacity to bless whatever is in front of us,
this is the enlightenment that is intimate with all things.*
—JACK KORNFIELD

*All finite things must go their finite way; I cannot bid the
merest moment, "Stay."*
—JAMES DILLET FREEMAN

Dear God, I set my heart on taking time to find something good in everything today. Even if there is an unexpected change, help me believe there is good in it. Help me polish my heart with the faith that frees me to make any needed changes. Help me to take a step to make one little change today for the sake of the strength that it builds in me.

Just last year Josh was a shy, soft-spoken eighth-grader. He dressed and acted conservatively and was the apple of his parents' eye. Now at a much bigger school with young people he has never seen before, he has transformed. His hair is dyed blue and spiked, he wears well-worn Levi's, cutoff T-shirts, and a spiked leather neck band and matching armband. His soft-spoken parents are beside themselves with the changes in their new, almost unrecognizable son. They are afraid—and praying.

My friend Ned just turned sixty and is finding his body changing in upsetting ways. He can't go for runs through the redwoods for miles the way he used to. He can't play competitive tennis matches anymore. His knees can't tolerate the stress. He told me, "I am angry. I had my routine down. I'd run every morning and play tennis two or three times a week with my friends. It's a real loss for me." No matter what his mind and heart want, his body is not cooperating and he feels powerless. He is afraid—and praying.

Ceil and Joe had been dating for seven years when they finally decided to get married. The children from their first marriages were on their own, and they knew this marriage was for keeps. They were excited about the new home they had designed together. But a little over a year later, Ceil began to be alarmed and afraid about changes she was seeing in Joe. He was spending long evening hours alone in his office and becoming distant even when they were together. He had lost interest in doing things socially, as well. Ceil was afraid that another divorce was on the horizon if this continued. She was afraid—and praying.

Our lives can become as unrecognizable to us as Josh had become to his parents. Change can walk through the door of our life, surprising, shocking, or baffling us. Even if we choose the change, it can turn our lives around and inside out.

Change is scary. But the truth is, it is an integral part of life. People can change from one day to the next, as can the circumstances of our lives. Just a simple sentence can change your life forever: "You've won the lottery." "I want a divorce." "You're pregnant." "You're fired."

Change is actually the way life lives itself. Whether joyous or terrifying, change is an opportunity to satisfy the yearning of our soul to know more of what is possible for us. It is an opportunity to expand our mind and grow in wisdom and power. If we will prayerfully swim with the current of the change rather than against it, we will find ourselves in the flow of Spirit that is directing our life to safe shores.

Hard as this may be to believe, there is a spiritual principle that promises that if we pronounce every experience good and hold to the thought that God can be found in it, by that mental attitude we will draw out the good that is incipient in it.

🌿 🍂

Strengthened by Visits to God

When I was young, my mother loved to go to downtown Chicago to shop, and she liked to bring me along. The shopping was fun but the highlight of the trip for both of us wasn't the stores, it was a visit to St. Peter's Basilica.

The church was sandwiched between two taller buildings on Madison Street, just a block from State Street and the shoppers' mecca. Its humble facade gave no clue to the astonishing beauty within its narrow walls. It was breathtaking to walk in off the noisy street to the pulsating silence that filled this immensity, with its high-vaulted ceiling, its variegated marble columns lining the depths of the sanctuary on both sides, small altars around the perimeter brightly lit with rows of small candles. We would quietly light a candle and then kneel in prayer for a while. My mom called this "making a visit." It always seemed to make Mom happier and lighter. I couldn't explain it then, but I always felt better too.

"Making visits" to God, whether praying in a quiet place or on a noisy street, whether praying in the silence of a numbing fear or in the racket of churning anger, builds a bridge of hope that helps us grow the faith needed to come out on the other end of the change stronger, wiser, surer, and with a greater capacity to love and be grateful.

A Practice for Facing Change

When you are facing or in the throes of change, focus your prayer on an aspect of God that addresses the kind of change you are experiencing. Let your need guide your request. If you *are experiencing a loss, perhaps speak your prayer into the strength or the love of God. For example, "God, give me the strength to walk through this." Or, "God, pour Your healing love into me." When you are afraid, you might call on the power of God, praying "God, give me the courage I need to do this." Think of the way in which you would like God to express in you. Imagine as you pray that you are breathing what you need into every thought. Also imagine that you are moving with the current of God's good plan.*

Recently I asked my friend Sandy how she was doing after her recent breakup with the man with whom she had been living for four years with the expectation of marriage. We had been spending a lot of time together and she always seemed so happy and upbeat. I wondered if all her cheerfulness was authentic. She said,

"I think I've been hiding from the anger and pain. I didn't even realize it, but I had a massage today and Marianne told me that she was sensing that my heart had been broken. That really touched something in me and I burst into tears that wouldn't quit."

Sometimes changes in our lives affect us so deeply that we bury the fear and pain, acting as if everything were okay prematurely. We are just not ready to face the change. When the change is a loss of someone or something that we hold dear, like Sandy, our souls grieve and often our minds disconnect so as not to experience the emotions that are a part of grieving. Yet the disconnect short-circuits healing, preventing us from integrating the experience in a way that enriches and beautifies the fabric of our soul and the tapestry of our lives.

In her deep sense of loss and betrayal, Sandy intensified her prayer life. She said, "In my prayers I asked God for understanding and to help me see what I was supposed to learn." Her prayer could have been "God, help me understand why this happened."

She began little by little to open her heart to finding something good in it. She claimed the good. It took months, but the moment arrived, not by coincidence, when she could say she was actually grateful that her relationship with Chad had ended. Would she have come to such peace and acceptance without prayer?

She doesn't think so.

Why We Resist Change

Sue Sikking, minister and author, writes: "We cannot stay in any one place and say: 'Here is where I want to be. I don't want anything else to happen to me. I want to be away from the fret and the worry.' This is not the way to happiness and contentment. Strange as it may seem, happiness, joy, contentment and victory belong to the overcomer."

And yet it is so human to want life and change on our own terms. We don't want to have to change ourselves or have changes come upon us unless we have guarantees, unless we are "ready," unless it's going to be relatively painless. We cannot grow or discover our true potential, though, without allowing ourselves to change and be changed for the better.

Sometimes the changes that life brings turn our lives upside down. Julie's once-thriving business was in the doldrums. She and her partner had invested in an elegant office space and hired a staff. Now they could barely make payroll and were going to have to let people go as well as change their lifestyle. They were angry and afraid. Their peaceful life had been turned upside down. They didn't want to let anyone go. They didn't want to have to press harder to make sales. They didn't want to have to change their lifestyle—the theater, dining out, great vacations.

Joan was resisting the change of her children moving out of the house because she was afraid of being alone. How did she resist? She was telling herself before it even happened how lonely she would be, how sad she would be, and how difficult life would be without the children at home anymore. She tried to sell both of them on choosing a school close to home, within easy driving distance. When a change frightens us, our first course of action is often to try to stop it. Joan was focused on her fears rather than on what might be best for her children.

Even when we know that a change is for the best, making it can be difficult. Even when the change is something we look forward to—a promotion at work, a marriage, a new home, a new car—there is a loss, a letting go of some kind. When we move on to a more promising job, we must still get through letting go of a job in which we may have found great fulfillment and companionship. When we divorce, we must let go of a lifestyle, and often certain friendships are lost as well.

Whatever the change, it is natural to feel an energetic resistance to letting go. We invested our creative energy, our intellectual and emotional energy, in the old way, and leaving it can be like pulling up an oak tree. The roots of the oak cling voraciously to the earth. Every memory will hold fast to the ground of consciousness in which it was planted. We ease the process of change and even grace the experience by praying it.

As James Dillet Freeman notes, the important thing to remember about a gift of prayer is that it changes us for the better:

> Prayer may bring you the fulfillment of your highest hopes and fondest dreams, but whether or not it does, prayer is valuable, not for the things it may bring you, but for the fact that you are praying. Prayer is valuable, not because it alters the circumstances and conditions of your life, but because it alters you. To pray is to feel your mind calming, your body relaxing, your spirit lightening, your heart lifting.

Crying Out Our Grief to the Great Heart of God

Last night I attended a wake for the father of a man in our congregation. Bob had called me earlier in the week to pray and talk about his dad and ask for help with giving the eulogy. He had been asked to do it and wasn't sure he was up to it. Bob and his father had been very close. "My father was at every baseball and football game I ever played," he said. "He has always been there for me. I don't know what I'm going to do without him here."

In the midst of his pain and fear, Bob did not run. He was willing to feel it all. I told him, "Bob, you are not alone in this. God will give you the words to speak." And then we prayed together. The prayer I prayed with him was an affirmation of God's protection, purpose, and provision: "What God has called you to do, God equips you to do." When I saw Bob at the visitation that night, I asked if he was ready for the funeral the next day. He smiled, and said, "Yes, I am. I know that I am not doing this alone."

Like Bob, you and I do not have to handle any change alone. If we can pray for help, trusting that the indwelling Divine is greater than the difficulty in any change, we will receive what we need from the great heart of God. In Paul's letter to the Philippians, he reassures them, "My God will supply all of your needs according to His riches." This is our reassurance as well. If we will lean on God in prayer, we will be given what we need and it will always be greater and, often, very different than we could have imagined.

The old Irish word for *lament* gave us the English word *keening*. Keening is the wail of the soul, those moans and groans that collapse the distances between heaven and earth. I first heard someone keen on the day my mother died.

Before making the drive from Gainesville to Clearwater, Florida, I called to talk with my dad. One of my sisters was already there and answered the phone. As we talked about arrangements, I could hear my father in the background making the most soulful, heart-wrenching sounds I had ever heard. My sister said that he had been up since 3:00 A.M. calling out to my mother through the distances, declaring his love. How healing, I thought. All of the love that he had not expressed through the years to my mom was coming now in a most primitive kind of prayer.

Sometimes the change we face is a loss that penetrates the depths of our being, splintering our soul and carrying off pieces of it, and all we can do in our pain is cry out to the great heart that receives our pain in a kind of loving embrace that allows us the space and the grace to be fully human and fully present to ourselves in a healing way.

Kathy finally made the decision to separate from her husband.

She had been putting it off for a long time, afraid of the change. Staying with him, though, had become more painful than the fear of leaving. She still loved her husband but found that their values and goals were constantly clashing. In her pain she cried out to the great heart of God for help to do what she believed she had to do. She joined a prayer group that supported her in prayer and encouraged her when the fear returned and she thought about going back to her husband. Today she can say something she never thought she would ever say: "This is the best thing that has ever happened to me." She came out of the boat of her well-anchored yet unhappy life, reaching out to God to become her new anchor. It worked for her and it will work for you.

Just think of how often people stay in marriages and jobs as their souls shrivel and their hearts harden—all so that they don't have to walk into the unknown.

It is important to remember, though, that every death offers us an opportunity to enter into the mystery of life and of our very soul to discover still more. Every death is the doorway to a new beginning and prayer gives us the strength to cross the threshold. But first we have to stop fighting the change and allow the current of the Divine to guide us through the uncharted waters and buoy our spirit until we reach the dry land of a new life.

Sometimes when I'm in the throes of a painful change, I get in the car, drive out onto the open road, roll up my windows, and begin to scream. It's my form of keening. I let my mind go to the depths of my pain and raise it up through screaming it out to God. I scream until there is no energy left to scream. I feel a release, and a sense of peace that passes all understanding washes through me.

The next time you are grieving the loss that any change brings, I invite you to find your own way of keening, of releasing the energy, being mindful that you are letting it go into the healing energy of God. It helps to make it physical. Throw rocks (being careful not to hit anyone or destroy property, of course!), work out, go for a run. Release your feelings to God. Find prayer support the way Kathy did.

Letting Go with Love

It was barely more than a year after my mother died that my brother, sisters, and I realized that my father's health had deteriorated drastically and that he could no longer live alone. He just didn't want to go on without my mother. After many phone calls, and two visits from his home in Texas to my father's home in Florida, my brother finally persuaded him to come live in Texas. Six months after the move, my father was diagnosed with colon cancer and given only a few months to live. He agreed to undergo a risky surgery in order to relieve the unbearable pain he was experiencing.

Two days after the surgery I received word that he might not make it through another day. I felt a sense of panic at the thought that he might die before I could get there. It was four hours by plane. As I agonized during the four hours in flight, I made a commitment to change my priorities. I had put off going sooner because of the sense of responsibility I felt to the class I was teaching. I had put it ahead of my need to be there as my father went through the dying process.

The ride from the airport to the hospital was the longest ride of my life. I prayed all the way, "God, please don't let Dad die before I get there. Please help Dad hang on." I called out to my father as if in prayer, "Dad, please don't die before I get there." I invested every ounce of energy I had in those beseeching prayers. I began to visualize arriving in time to cradle my dad and tell him how much I loved him and what a good job he did as a parent.

My sister-in-law met the van as it pulled up to the hospital entrance. The first and only words out of my mouth were "Is he gone?" She said "No," and I took her hand and started running.

As I entered the hospital room, the first thing I saw was my brother Jimmy at the foot of the hospital bed, crying. I had never seen him cry. My heart sank. I looked over at my dad. His eyes were open but blank. He had an oxygen mask on and his mouth was open. I screamed "No!" Jimmy said, "He just took his last breath as you came in. He waited for you." Just as I had envisioned on the flight, I held my dad for a long time, singing his favorite songs into his ear. I sang his songs like prayers to carry his soul back home and into the heart of his Creator. It helped me let go. The great heart of God is great enough to carry us through every kind of change.

Jimmy had so much unfinished business with my dad—the times my dad wasn't there for him; the times his discipline was so harsh; the things Jim didn't say about how hard that was and the things he didn't say about how much he admired and loved Dad. He allowed himself to say those things as he kept watch during those last days in the hospital. He told Dad that he had been a good father and thanked him for the good example he set as a father and husband. Jim said, "I told him I was sorry for being impatient with him these past few months when he wouldn't eat right or take his medicine. He took my hand and told me he loved me and that it was all right and not to worry." In those moments all the gaps in their relationship were bridged and Jim's heart was healed. Both Jim and my dad spoke from hearts that were at one with the great heart and all of their prayers through the years were answered.

There is no change that prayer can't help us handle. There is no gulf that prayer can't build a bridge to heal.

Make a Space for Grace

I recently facilitated a women's retreat. Our theme was "Discerning Your Path." A good number of women there were at a crossroads in their lives, knowing that something was calling them, knowing that they wanted something more in their lives. They were looking for answers, for clarity of direction, and, more important, for the courage to make the changes that were barely discernible hints and whispers from deep inside.

Many really knew what they had to do but were afraid to do it. How do I leave a career that has given me my identity? Where will I go and what will I do? How do I leave this well-paying but unsatisfying job without knowing what to do next? What do I do with my life after forty years of marriage to the same man? How do I go on alone?

When we discern spiritually, we seek God's will, nothing more, nothing less, nothing else. We pray to see the great possibility in the change.

One woman, Alicia, told of being diagnosed with breast cancer and of going into prayer and meditation after the results came back positive. She said, "I was at home alone and lit candles and began to pray. The room became full of energy and I felt the presence of angels, the ones I had left behind when I was seven. I asked in prayer that I be spared long enough to raise my fourteen-year-old daughter.

"That night, just after meditating, I was feeling pretty doomed by all of this. I had a vision, though, of being in another dimension, helping those who had passed over from suicide and violence or had died feeling unworthy of God's love. I realize right now, today, that my path is to walk in total faith, as an instrument of healing. I have always been a nurse, but now it has a whole new meaning for me."

Prayer opens us to such revelations, bringing a sense of meaning to the changes that life brings. It makes a space for grace. Alicia knew that whatever time was given to her would be made meaningful. She was graced with a new vision for her life.

During the retreat we talked about living a path with heart, growing in our capacity to bless whatever comes to us. That led to the question of suffering and a discussion about the distinctions between pain and suffering. We talked about pain being a part of the human experience, the changes that upset our sense of well-being, peace, and security. Then what is suffering? If I am in pain, am I suffering? The pain of our experience may be excruciating physically, mentally, emotionally, or spiritually, but suffering is the result of fighting the pain and its cause rather than leaning into it and breathing the healing power of God into it through prayer.

There was an article in the paper last week about a young and beautiful sixteen-year-old girl who, while surfing with some friends off the coast of southern California, had her right arm torn off by a shark. One moment she was happily resting on her surfboard and the next moment she was yanked off the board by a shark that had grabbed hold of her dangling arm. She spoke with the most incredible equanimity about how she was not going to let this terrible accident depress her or stop her. She said that she might not surf competitively again but that she would be back up on her surfboard soon. Was she in pain physically and emotionally? Yes. Was she suffering? No.

As we pray for acceptance and breathe God into our difficult experiences, God's grace transforms pain and suffering into triumph and we experience a resurrection out of darkness into the light of meaning and the will to live well.

Remember, the God who created you has a plan for your life and it's a good one. As God said, speaking through the prophet Jeremiah, "I know the plans I have for you, plans to prosper you and to give you a hope and a future." To hold the vision that the

Divine in each of us is inexorably seeking to be matured and expressed through each change, no matter how difficult, and that in each change there is a greater good seeking to be born, is to hold the key to triumphant living. It is the key to true power. Praying from this perspective opens the door to healing and to the good we seek.

With each change, we have the option to pause and choose: How will I take this change and what will I make of it—a burden or a blessing? Will I allow it to devastate me or motivate me? Will I see it as an insurmountable problem with God or the universe against me or as a poignant opportunity to demonstrate the power of God in my life and me? Reflect for a moment on the changes in your life in the last five years alone. Which were of the most impact and how? How were you changed by the changes?

If, in the midst of change, you can remember to pause and pray, making a space for grace, the grace of the living God will minister to you, encouraging your heart and renewing your spirit. The Apostle Paul wrote to disheartened people who were allowing the difficult conditions in Rome to mold their minds and shape their lives: "Do not be conformed to this world but be transformed by the renewal of your mind. . . ." Instead of letting the changes determine our thinking, in prayer we let the grace of God shape our thinking into hope and a vision of greater good to come and inspire us to meaningful action.

Practices for Handling Change

1. **Let it be transformed.** Any time doubt, worry, fear, or anger come up in you regarding a change, give it to God, the great Alchemist, to transform into something useful. Turn your thoughts back to something positive and nourishing.

2. Try Centering Prayer:

* Take a comfortable position. Close your eyes and focus your attention on your breathing, letting go as much as possible of all thoughts.

* Stir up faith in and love for God, Who abides at the center of your being. To stir up faith, recall the times that things have worked out in your life beyond what you could have imagined or arranged. Take time to reflect on the many changes you have successfully and effectively come through in spite of how monumentally difficult they may have been. In the midst of turmoil, it is so easy to forget the many times we have confronted and mastered difficulties. Take a minute to consider the good that came out of those changes that you may have wanted to run from or approached kicking and screaming. Pray a prayer of thanks and let the memory of your success inform any current difficult changes.

* Choose a sacred word that directs your attention Godward. The word could be God, Jehovah, Shalom. It might be love, peace, or light. Pick a name for the Divine or a word that is an attribute of the Divine. The important thing is that it is meaningful to you.

* Introduce the word to your imagination and let it be gently present. As thoughts arise, gently return your attention to the sacred word. Accept peacefully all that comes to your mind, but return again and again to the sacred word that takes you back to God.

* Try to stay with this prayer for ten to twenty minutes.

3. Visualize the good you seek beyond the change you are experiencing (job change, move, loss of relationship, health changes). See the best possible outcome. Affirm it.

Say a prayer of thanks for the good coming into your life. This is a prayer of faith, for you are willing to believe before you see. It is also affirmative prayer, because you insist on believing in the good before you see it.

Affirmations:

I trust God to bring me through and gift me too.

I am magnetic to the good I seek and it is magnetic to me.

God is in this change with a blessing that far exceeds the difficulty.

God strengthens me and guides my every step.

Prayers

Dear God, help me recognize that there is within me a perfect self; a self that is not weak but strong; that is not limited but limitless; that is not small but great. I am willing to wear the mantle of Your magnificence. I invoke Your light. I receive Your grace and move to a new place and new freedom.

Dear God, I come to You today to be shown the way to believe the best, hope for the best, trust in the best, and let go of the rest. When doubt fills my heart and confidence slips away, help me stay close to You. Give me the courage to test my wings that I might know the fullness of the potential You have given me.

Dear God, You are the great Alchemist Who can change me in the twinkling of an eye. You are the enchantment that lures me into faithful action and fruitful endeavors. I open the windows of my heart to You now. Come with Your bountiful gifts and bless me. Change the shadow of any darkness in me into the beauty of Your light. Put Your hand on my worries and turn them to the gold of wisdom.

Dear God, I think of You as the Source of all hope and I really need that now. It feels like the light in my heart has gone out with this loss. I feel empty and confused. Come minister to me in all the ways You know I need Your presence and power right now. I let go into Your healing love all the pain I feel and hold fast to faith in Your all-providing response to my call.

Dear God, I thank You that You help me accept this change and use it for good.

Dear God, I don't know what the future holds but I know that You hold my future. Keep my mind and heart steady and optimistic as You guide me through this change. Keep me from forcing solutions and grasping at easy answers. Just for today help me focus on making this day a very good one.

Chapter 7

Partnering with Grace:

Prayers for Healing

Health is the normal condition of man and of all creation. We find that there is an omnipresent principle of health pervading all living things. Health, real health, is from within and does not have to be manufactured (from outside). Health is the very essence of Being.
—CHARLES FILLMORE

Loving Lord, I come to You today asking that You show me the way to be healed and made whole and free. Shine Your light to the depths of my soul, dissolving any darkness and revealing Your goals for my life. Shine Your love on the wounds and scars, healing each one. Make me like new, a reflection of You and Your Love that knows no bounds. Shine the light of Your life in my body, making it a spotless temple where Your spirit dwells in freedom and fullness. Amen.

Ruth's life looked to be on an upswing. She had reconciled with her daughter after some painful years of estrangement. She was finally able to buy a home, one that she loved, and she had a new and challenging job that she was excited about. I hadn't seen her this ebullient in the five years I had known her.

Then her world came crashing down. A routine checkup on a thyroid condition revealed a mass in her colon that turned out to be malignant. It required immediate surgery. Ruth's shock turned to terror.

The realization that her life was at stake began a turnaround in Ruth that amazed her family and friends—and led her to develop a healing consciousness.

Never one to ask for help for herself, she began to reach out for prayer support, creating a circle of prayer partners. She made a searching inventory of her life and her values, considering what changes needed to be made, and set about making them. She began by cleaning up the past, most especially her relationship with her mother, whom she had hated most of her life. She knew that to truly heal she had to find a way to forgive her mother. She spent an afternoon with me talking about and writing down all the things she held against her until she could think of no more. Then with a prayer she burned her list as a sign of releasing every resentment.

We were all shocked when after recovering from the surgery she joined a fitness center and actually went three times a week. This was radical for a woman who proudly declared that she never exercised because it would cause her to sweat. She started getting massages, and even pedicures and manicures regularly. She deepened her spiritual life and practice as well, volunteering at church each week, joining the prayer team to support others in prayer. In those months following the surgery, she would laughingly remark, "This staying healthy is a full-time job." And she was right.

Life is so fragile, and we never know how many days are before us. A diagnosis can change a life forever. A change of heart can end a relationship. A change in the economy can end a career.

On top of that, the incredibly fast pace of our lives too often leaves us dazed at the end of the day. We become driven by tasks and work, inundated with information that we are asked to process at record speed. Even balancing our lives requires diligence. In such a frenetic environment, it is easy to go unconscious about what we put into our being—spirit, soul, and body. In fact, mindless intake of food, TV, movies, alcohol, drugs, shopping, sex, gambling, and even conversation seems to be a way to unhook ourselves from the pressures and the pace.

Putting our spiritual health first is the key. Taking time to pray brings us back to ourselves and to an awareness of our inner ecology. Prayer harmonizes the environment of our inner world so that we can approach and engage our outer world consciously and effectively. It puts us in touch with what really matters to us. Then we don't need a diagnosis like the one Ruth received to awaken us to the preciousness of each day and the people whose lives we touch.

Letting prayer be a priority health practice leads us to an awe and appreciation for the life we've been given. Prayer helps us love life because it deepens our relationship with the Giver of life. Loving life and the very idea of health and wholeness begins a process of being empowered to give up what depletes our health and zest for living. It all begins by developing a healing consciousness.

True Healing

The word *heal* is derived from the root word *hal*, which is defined as sound, healthy, whole. Healing, then, is more than "curing" the body. Healing restores us to integrity, soundness, and wholeness. It is the creative activity of the energy of life and love. Healing dissolves the obstacles to peace and joy, and so it begins with our thinking. Step by step, thought by thought, we seek to align with all that is life-giving and all that softens our heart into love and compassion. With every thought we seek alignment with God as the creative principle of life, love, wisdom, joy, and peace. God is the very essence of health and wholeness. Through prayer we engage the power of God to cocreate with us a state of health and wholeness.

No matter what we need healing for, prayer is the conduit for the energy of healing. As we pray for healing, the most helpful thing we can do is see and affirm the desired condition. We breathe in the energy of divine life as the light that overcomes any darkness. This light knows what to do and needs only our gracious invitation.

In Chapter 3, I told the story of the cofounder of Unity, Myrtle Fillmore, who was healed of tuberculosis at a time when the disease was nearly always fatal. In fact, Myrtle had been told she had only six months to live when she began a rigorous, systematic spiritual practice. I say "rigorous" because she spent hours each day in prayer. She systematically prayed into every part of her body. She said:

> It flashed upon me that I might talk to the life in every part of my body . . . I began to teach my body and got marvelous results. . . . I told my limbs that they were active and strong. . . . I went to all the life centers in my body and spoke

words of Truth to them—words of strength and power. I asked their forgiveness for the foolish, ignorant course that I had pursued in the past when I condemned them and called them weak, inefficient, and diseased. I did not become discouraged at their being slow to wake up but kept right on, both silently and aloud, declaring the words of Truth until the organs responded.

While the mind and soul are healed through prayer, the body may not always be cured in the medical sense. Myrtle was healed and cured. My friend Ruth was healed and not cured. In the final days of her life, Ruth told me that she was happier than she had ever been and that she had never felt so much love. She died with a smile on her face, looking radiant and years younger.

As we step outside the medical model of healing, a whole new world of possibilities and resources opens to us. We can explore ideas and practices that restore all levels of our being: spirit, soul, and body.

What is true is that if we can conceive of an idea the reality of that idea already exists in potential. As we focus the power of our mind on a spiritual truth, the truth begins to manifest in and through us. Praying for healing of spirit, soul, or body is the activity of partnering with grace, the activity of God. In prayer we go beyond the level of the symptom to the divine idea of life, focusing on the most beautiful possibility that we can imagine. In this we are aligning with the organic, dynamic Spirit of God, often called grace. Grace is God's love in action and God as love can only be life giving and life enhancing.

As the medical intuitive Caroline Myss points out in *Anatomy of the Spirit*, a cure is when the physical progression of an illness has been successfully controlled or abated. It is more passive than active on the part of the person experiencing the "cure." Healing, however, is active and includes "investigating one's attitudes, memories, and beliefs with a desire to release all negative patterns that prevent one's full emotional and spiritual recovery. Healing includes beginning to use energy for the creation of love, self-esteem, and health."

My father wasn't cured of colon cancer, but his spirit and soul were healed as he found with my brother a willingness to surrender into being cared for, into being loved just for himself, just the way he was. Caregivers of AIDS patients talk of witnessing the transformations that take place as the patients experience an outpouring of love from the people around them. Taking in such love does something to heal their spirit in a way that turns their viewpoint from anger, self-pity, and hopelessness to one of joy, strength, courage, and faith. These experiences demonstrate over and over that curing the body is not requisite for true healing to occur. And yet, the spirit of life itself in us insists that we pray for healing of spirit, soul, and body.

The divine idea of life is inherent in every cell and atom of our body. In prayer we work with this incipient intelligence and substance of life. We seek in prayer to create a loving relationship with all parts of our being, our thoughts, emotions, perceptions, attitudes, and bodies, much as Myrtle Fillmore did, knowing that all things are possible with God.

Annie was critically injured in an automobile accident, with broken bones and punctured organs throughout her body. She was paralyzed from the neck down and she was told that she would never walk again. But Annie had been a spiritual seeker for many years and had a deep understanding of the power of prayer thinking. She began a dedicated practice of prayer that included visualizing every bone in her body, every organ and vein, every muscle and ligament, in their healed, whole condition.

She carried this faith through seventeen surgeries and three years in the hospital. She believed in the possibility before she saw it. Today she walks, swims, and dances. The only residual effect is a slight limp, but even that is dissipating. She told me, "I never believed I couldn't be healed. I knew I could. I talked to my body every day. I loved it and appreciated it. I would sing prayers to it. I was busy every day in healing."

Becoming Spiritually Fit

Jon had a spotty work record, had been struggling with an addiction to alcohol, and had just gone through a very painful divorce when we met. He had been fired often enough, and had been in and out of enough recovery programs, that he was willing to try a new way. Now back in recovery, he felt a glimmer of hope. "I don't want to mess up this time," he said. "Tell me what books to read and what classes to take because I have got to learn to keep my thinking straight." We talked about a "spiritual fitness plan." He started with a beginning prayer class and continued taking prayer classes until ready to become a part of the prayer team that prayed with people after Sunday services. As one of our most passionate spokespersons for the healing power of prayer, he continually encourages people to get into our prayer classes and get serious about their prayer life. He also facilitates a prayer circle and is one of our key volunteer leaders. Think about your own spiritual fitness plan. What would you be willing to do?

It was Einstein who said that you cannot solve a problem at the level of thinking that got you there. We have to notch up our thinking, to view our circumstances from a higher perspective. That perspective is a spiritual perspective. Through a committed prayer practice, a door in our thinking opens to view our circumstances from a solution-oriented perspective.

Creating a healing consciousness may not be a new notion, but today we actually have scientific evidence that the quality of our thinking directly affects our health—spirit, soul, and body. In other words, it is possible for us to change the conditions of our lives and our bodies by changing the conditions of our minds.

Try the spiritual workout plan that follows. You will be amazed at the results.

Step 1. *Believe in the possibility.*

The whole of our being seeks health and well-being, whether of spirit, soul, or body, because something in us tells us that health and well-being are normal. You can take the first step toward healing by becoming receptive to the *possibility* and releasing any beliefs to the contrary. For example, the belief that we inherit illness, physical limitations, or mental traits like depression, that they "run in the family," is very strong both inside and outside the medical community. Yet the universal, spiritual principle that as we change our mind so we change our experience suggests that we can change the belief that we inherit illness, with the result that we change our experience. We do not inherit the illness. We inherit the belief.

I've heard people say "I have bad genes" as the way to explain addiction issues like eating or drinking. I've heard the same kind of thing about inheriting certain dispositions. But current genetic research suggests that while we may inherit a potential, we are not doomed or imprisoned by it.

For example, a friend of mine comes from a family where being overweight is considered an inherited trait. He decided as a young man that he was not going to be overweight. He made choices that supported that desire—he ate healthy foods, cut out sugar, and exercised regularly. Now, years later, he is lean and in great physical shape. By choosing not to own the family belief that overweight was the normal state for him, he *changed* the belief and lived from the new belief, and the result is a trim, healthy body.

As you pray, believing in the possibility before you see it, you partner with grace, which is the mystery of the activity of God in your life. Each time he was asked to heal someone, the great healer Jesus Christ said, "Your faith has made you well."

As you do the spiritual work of developing a healing consciousness through prayer, you practice believing in the possibility by letting your thoughts and actions be faithful prayers.

Step 2. *Become receptive to healing.*

The second step in developing a healing consciousness is becoming receptive to healing. This is not as easy as it might seem. It requires acknowledging and actually embracing what needs healing, which is contrary to what comes naturally to us: ordinarily we resist and fight what we don't want and don't like. However, nothing can change as long as we fight and resist.

Of the 3,500 calls a day that come to Silent Unity, a 24/7 prayer ministry, the majority are requests for prayers for healing. Reaching out for prayer or in prayer is a way of affirming that you are receptive.

Suzanne, a beautiful sixteen-year-old, has an eating disorder that is seriously compromising her immune system. Recently, she developed pneumonia and was no sooner over that than she had strep throat. Her mother has talked to her. Her doctor has talked to her. So far, to no avail. Suzanne is not yet receptive to healing.

Receptivity to being healed calls us to be willing to let go of attitudes, beliefs, and behaviors that block the kind of health and wholeness we desire. We need to be willing to change and be changed. Even with a common cold we need to be willing to rest, take medicine, drink lots of liquids. When we are receptive, what needs to be changed or released can be revealed. Your prayer here can be, "Lord, I am willing to be willing." Then later, "Lord, let there be light. Let me know what I need to know, see what I need to see, so that I can do what needs to be done."

Keeping our hearts receptive is a lifelong spiritual task. We must be willing to take action each day as negative emotions come up—and they always do—to release them to God and refocus our thinking on life-giving thoughts.

Step 3. *Be forgiving.*

Forgiveness is central to healing. In Chapter 4 we considered forgiveness as an essential practice in developing and maintaining healthy, harmonious relationships. It is just as essential to developing a healing consciousness and being part of a spiritual fitness program. In order to heal, we need to forgive the condition, realizing at the same time that we did not inherit it and God is not punishing us with it.

Friends brought a man who was paralyzed to Jesus to be healed one day. Jesus, seeing their faith, said, "My friend, your sins are forgiven" to effect the healing. The scribes and Pharisees, who in no way believed in the power of forgiveness to heal, accused him of misusing the power of God. Jesus responded by saying, "Which is easier to say, 'Your sins are forgiven' or 'Rise and walk'?" He then addressed the paralytic, saying, "I say to you, rise, take up your bed and go home." And the man did.

A modern spiritual look at the "seven deadly sins" and their derivatives is helpful here. It is important to understand that sin is a misunderstanding of spiritual law and spiritual truth. In our misunderstanding we make mistakes, sometimes small, sometimes huge, about what will bring us health and wholeness. These mistakes always damage our overall vitality and sense of well-being.

Once we realize our mistakes and become willing to change, we are ready to experience release and an immense and indescribable freedom through forgiveness. It is a process of cleaning the home of our consciousness on a daily basis. When we notice any of these feelings showing up, the first step is to have compassion. All of them are survival modes of living, which we somehow came to believe helped us survive in our world. The next step is to give them to God. Let them go into God and change the thought or action. Think of something you are grateful for. Do something nice for someone. Do something nice for yourself.

Seven Health Robbers

 • **False pride** *causes us to isolate from fear of being wrong or being rejected. In forgiving, we can ask ourselves: Do I isolate, make myself and others wrong, refuse to ask for help or even admit that I need help?*

 • **Anger** *is misused when we "stuff" or ignore it, or when we act it out on ourselves and others. Look and see. Do I stuff my anger, refuse to acknowledge it? Do I dump it on others rather than seek what is under the anger and address that issue?*

 • **Envy** *is a substitute for taking responsible action on behalf of our own dreams and desires. Do I think that everyone else gets the breaks? That others have it easier than I?*

 • **Gluttony** *is unquenchable overconsumption. It can be attempting to control others or situations to have it our way. In addition to overeating to fill emotional holes, it can be overconsuming attention, praise, or approval. Does it seem as though I never get enough appreciation or attention? Do I eat when my body is not hungry but my soul is? Do I have a hard time letting others shine? Do I feel inadequate in any way— not smart enough, popular enough, good enough?*

 • **Jealousy** *is close to envy, but it is more related to a basic distrust of God, self, and life, than to wanting what others have. It rises from fear that something you have may be*

taken from you. It can show up as showing off, bragging and boasting, making others wrong, putting others down. Do I talk negatively about others to make myself look good? Do I always seek to be better, do better, look better?

● Lust goes way beyond sexual desire; it is a driven kind of thinking in which we become obsessed about what we do not have, craving it. We can lust after power, attention, appreciation, position, or money—anything we think will fill an emptiness in us. Am I always jockeying for the spotlight? Do I always need to have more clothes, a bigger home? Do I put others' needs at the mercy of my own?

● Sloth is a persistent laziness about how we care for ourselves and our lives. It is poor stewardship of all that has been given us. Do I incessantly procrastinate or abdicate taking care of myself and my resources? Do I hope that others will recognize my talents but fail to develop them myself?

Enfolded in the idea of forgiveness is the activity of accepting the facts and allowing a vibrant compassion to connect with the condition. In the case of conditions or circumstances—on the job, in the home, in the body—after accepting them, we ask God to work in and through us to heal what needs to be healed. As all spiritual masters have taught, we ask God to love our "enemies" through us, whether our enemy is a disease, a person, or a job. We turn then to investing our creative energy in thoughts that enhance our health and well-being. Forgiveness heals the disconnect with Spirit, our life force.

Another essential part of this practice is self-forgiveness. We are called to forgive our humanness, our moods, our negative emotions, our self-criticism. Forgiveness offers the gift of inner peace, healing the recurring wars within us. We take sides against ourselves long before we take sides against others. In prayer we ask the activity of the love of God, grace, to help us accept our own inner struggles as they come up, to transform them into something useful. We give self-reproach to the creative power of love to heal as we turn our attention to what makes our heart and soul sing. We begin to live in the answer, the healthy, whole condition.

Three Forgiveness Practices

1. *For one month, before bed, do a kneeling prayer (kneeling in prayer is miraculous) giving thanks for your body and all the ways it serves you. Speak words of gratitude to it.*

2. *This week make a practice of sending loving thoughts to any condition, circumstance, or relationship that needs healing.*

3. *If one of the seven deadly sins shows up for work, tell it that you won't be needing it anymore, that you have found a better way. Then do a good deed or think of something you are grateful for.*

The last step in the forgiveness process is the action of amending. With a new taste of peace and freedom, we commit to changing our ways. Whatever our situation, we pray for the courage and strength to respond to it in new, healthy ways. Instead of allowing life-depleting thoughts, words, and actions to run us, we release them with compassion. We turn our thoughts to high-level, noble things. This is performing a good deed for ourselves and others.

As we practice forgiveness, we are healed. When we heal ourselves, we heal others.

Step 4. *Be passionate about the divine idea of health and wholeness: feed it and feel it.*

Falling in love with the idea of health and wholeness and practicing feeding it, feeling it, and expressing it is one of the most potent life-enhancing practices. Loving the idea of health and wholeness is loving God and yourself. What can you do today that excites you? What can you do that energizes you? If you enjoy music, do you have a concert on your schedule? If you love theater, do you have tickets to a play? If sports are your thing, do you have a plan to watch or participate this week? If reading warms your heart, do you have a good book and a plan to curl up with it tonight?

Me? I love spa experiences. So I spend time looking at spa magazines and make a point of going to at least one new spa a year.

My son loves fishing and all sports. He plays on a baseball, football, or basketball team so that year-round he is doing what he loves to do. He has a group of friends who love to fish too. They take fishing trips each year.

One of my friends who used to be really heavy got sick and tired of being sick and tired one day. She had been talking for years about how she just couldn't seem to lose weight. The trouble was that she was feeding the problem she wanted to be rid of instead of the good that she desired.

Finally she did something different. She joined a fitness center, got a trainer, and changed her diet. Today she looks great and is passionate about the idea of health. When I talked to her recently, she was crestfallen. Her fitness center had closed. "I was so disappointed," she said. "I love that place and I loved going there." She was planning to find a new one within the week. This is being passionate about health and wholeness, feeding it and feeling it.

Fall in love with what makes you feel healthy and program it into your life. It will feed your whole being.

Step 5. *Practice expressing love and appreciation.*

I was preparing a memorial service for a well-known and beloved colleague recently and called his wife to talk about what she wanted said and done. She talked about all the people who had come to her to say what a wonderful man her husband was and what a difference he had made in their lives. Then she paused, and said, "Why do people wait until someone is gone to say how much they loved him?"

So often we feel needy and want or wait for or even expect others to love and appreciate us first. Often we go into automatic drive through our days, hardly stopping to appreciate anything or anyone.

This step asks you to express love and appreciation on a daily basis whether you feel like it or not: to make appreciation a prayer practice. You will find that the act of appreciating another is actually energizing. When we reach out to be a blessing to another, we are immediately enlivened and enveloped in a sense of well-being.

In fact numerous studies have shown that our health and sense of well-being improve remarkably through the practices of expressing love and appreciation. It is being clinically demonstrated that the happiest people in the world are those who love fully and fearlessly and feel and express appreciation consistently and lavishly.

On days when I feel most needy and most unloved and unlovable, I pray for the willingness to reach out to another. I give my neediness to God and ask something like: "God, who can I love for You today?" A name always comes. I go to the phone and call the person just to see how they are and let them know I care. Or I sit down and write a note to someone telling them in a specific way how much I appreciate them. This is one of the surest, simplest ways to feel blessed and energized.

Step 6. Find a way to serve.

Finding a way to serve practically guarantees a healing consciousness. It is one of the ways that the creative principle of love expresses itself. When we get outside of our own self-absorption, we engage the power of the Divine in a life-giving, healing way. Serving is the practice of asking ourselves, "What can I give here?" rather than "What can I get here?" With this intention, we not only heal ourselves, we become a healing presence as well. Selfless service is prayer in action.

Twelve-step programs make service essential. The founders of Alcoholics Anonymous discovered that in order to stay sober, they had to reach out to help others. Everyone in AA is encouraged to be of service as soon as possible by helping out at meetings—making coffee, setting up the room, emptying ashtrays. Every little act of service is considered an investment in their sobriety. The spiritual principle of service heals, whether in a twelve-step program or not. We all need to recover from something that hinders our sense of worth, freedom, vitality, peace, or joy.

The principle of service is ancient wisdom. It is love in action, and love is the great healer.

Albert Schweitzer said, "I don't know what your destiny will be, but one thing I know: the only ones among you who will be really happy are those who have sought and found how to serve."

Everyone had given up on Bill. Having been through twenty-four treatment facilities for alcoholism, he was considered a hopeless drunk. But then in treatment program number twenty-five, he met a man who was able to teach him the value of service. Sid ran the treatment center with a fierce insistence on daily service. Within the first few days in treatment, Bill was cooking and serving breakfast to thirty other alcoholics and drug addicts. He did it grudgingly at first—no smiles and no conversation. But then as the days wore on, his demeanor changed. He'd be whistling while vacuuming or kidding the cook when it was Bill's turn to set the table. This time after treatment, Bill not only stayed sober, he became an inspiration to hundreds of newcomers. And he could always be seen serving in some way at meetings.

Sally came to church every Sunday, sitting in the last row and leaving as soon as church was over. She tells the story, "I was so lonely and scared. I didn't want anyone to talk to me. I just wanted to be left alone. People were really nice to me, though, and I kept hearing about becoming involved. One day after service I went to the activities table. I had no intention of signing up for anything, but Judy was standing there and invited me to join her group, the Commitment Card team. When I heard the word 'commitment,' I almost broke out in a cold sweat. I said yes and it was the best thing I ever did." Sally shared this story one year later on a Sunday morning at church in front of the whole congregation. Why? She was now a team leader and inviting people to get into service.

The gifts we have been given by our Creator are not for us alone. We are meant to use our gifts to bless others' lives, as well as our own. Jesus said, "You are the light of the world. Let your light so shine that others may see the good that you do and give glory to God." There is a light in you that shines as your gifts and talents. Sharing them in the spirit of service not only multiplies them; shining your light helps others find the light in themselves. Sid took Bill under his wing and helped him see the light in himself.

Gandhi counseled his followers: "If you can't love the Viceroy, or Sir Winston Churchill, start with your wife, or your husband or your children. Try to put their welfare first and your own last every minute of the day, and let the circle of your love expand from there. . . ." We know that Gandhi spent hours in prayer to create this kind of healing consciousness. We know that the Buddha and Jesus Christ spent hours, even days, in prayer to create the healing consciousness that they possessed. Their intention in all was to be the healing expression of the Divine in the world.

Even a simple prayer asking to be an instrument of peace and loving-kindness before a conversation or interaction is a way of serving God.

Step 7. *Practice realization.*

Through the power of prayer, our mind is clothed in the energy of wholeness and well-being. Persistently holding thoughts of health and practicing healthy ways create healing. We become one with these ideas, ultimately embodying them. We become what we have been praying for. Our focused attention to the intention creates its reality.

Realization is the internal experience of crossing the chasm between a need for healing and the assurance of its fulfillment. It is knowing that the work is already done. In the Creation story we find that on the seventh day God called all that he had done good, and rested.

Think about a simple example like a time when you cut your finger slicing a roast. You knew what to do. You washed the cut, made sure it was clean, maybe put an antiseptic on it and then a Band-Aid. Then you let go and went about your business, confident that healing was taking place and soon the cut would be closed up. This is realization.

Pray until you have an inner conviction that your work is done, that "it is finished." Then let go and know that all is well. Feel it. Claim it—even before you see it done.

Practices for
Partnering with Grace

- Create a picture of health and well-being in your mind through gathering pictures of health, vitality, and joy. Picture yourself healthy, whole, loving, and happy. Enjoy it in your mind first. Then create a treasure map. Paste the pictures and words that speak of vitality, joy, and health on a poster board. Put it where you will see it daily.

- Pray for guidance in what needs to be changed in your health practices and listen to what Spirit reveals. Take action.

- Pray each day to be of service, making your first thought be *What can I contribute here?*

- Find a place to be in service in addition to the job for which you are paid.

- Spend time in prayer each night forgiving yourself for any mistakes, forgiving your body, forgiving everything and everyone.

- Each week send a note of appreciation to someone you care about and who makes a difference in your life.

Be of good cheer. The intelligence that created your body knows how to heal it. Get still, relax, turn your attention to the sustaining life forces within your organism.

—Charles Fillmore, Teach Us to Pray

Affirmations:

My entire being is healthy, whole, loving, and happy.

I give my attention to loving, and loving gives me new life.

The more I express my love and appreciation the better I feel.

Prayers

Lord of life and water that quenches all thirsts, come fill the cup of my life with You. Come quench the thirsting of my soul. Reassure me that no scar is too deep, no wrong too great, no dream too late for You to minister to and bless. Come, Lord, I am ready and willing.

Dear God, I come to You today asking that You open the way to a deep, rich relationship with You. Touch me with Your loving heart that I might love deeply and fearlessly. Search me and root out my fears and everything else unlike love. Let me find shelter in Your warm embrace, released from the worries that race in my mind. Melt the walls. Heal the hurts and bind the wounds and let me know the heaven of Your love in the earth of my life today.

Dear God, I come to You today with a mind for renewal. Inspire me to send the roots of my life deep into the soil of life's enduring values that I might grow toward the great destiny You have set for me. Help me to create heaven in the earth of my life, a clear and passionate heart, a soaring spirit, a vital, balanced body, a dream to live for, and Your guidance to live by.

Dear God, for all my healing needs, let me believe that nothing is too big or too small or impossible. Let me see it all with eyes of faith and from a heart of enthusiasm for the possible.

Lord, sometimes of myself I can't forgive and don't even want to forgive. Today is one of those days. So I give all of the fear and hurt that is wrapped up in my anger to You. I trust that You know what to do to heal me into forgiveness and I am willing.

Dear God, help me take people less for granted. Help me notice the little kindnesses and say thank you. Remind me to express love more often. Especially help me express love and take time to appreciate others when I am most needy.

Lord, help me to keep a mind of service in all I do today. Help me to listen with care and respond patiently and gently.

Chapter 8

Living the Abundant Life:

Prayers for Prosperity

True riches and real prosperity are in the understanding that there is an omnipresent substance from which all things come and that by the action of our minds we can unify ourselves with that substance so that the manifestations that come from it will be in line with our desires and needs.
—CHARLES FILLMORE, *Prosperity*

Dear God, I see Your abundance all around me—the star-filled sky, the astonishing variety and abundance in earth and sea and human beings. Inventiveness and creativity are evidenced everywhere. Let my inner eyes see such abundant and beautiful possibilities for my life. Help me keep my focus on all the good in my life and in the world and let this focus expand my horizons to embrace still more of Your abundant goodness in my life. Amen.

My son, Ed, had left messages on all my phones—office, home, and cell—so I knew something important was on his mind. When I finally was able to get back to him, he started talking about his recent visit to Florida, where he saw relatives he hadn't seen in over twenty years. He got around to talking about how he'd also seen my sister and brother-in-law on their recent trip out to California to visit their sons, but I was pretty sure that just catching up wasn't the main reason for his call.

There was a pause as he began to tell me how my sister and her husband were helping one of their sons financially, paying his rent when he ran short, sending a little cash in the mail regularly. I could hear anxiety rising in his voice as he told the story. He wanted help too. "I got a bill for twenty thousand dollars today for my school loan," he said, "and I don't know how I am going to pay it. I feel like I have been in debt all my life. I'm finally close to getting my truck paid off. I only owe two thousand dollars, and now this."

How often we say that to ourselves: Things were going so well and *now this*—an unexpected bill, a job loss, a scary diagnosis, a serious breach in a significant relationship—and our sense of security and well-being goes out the window.

Ed had gone to college out of high school but dropped out after two years, telling himself that he would go back after he made some money. As the years passed, his dream of finishing never died, but . . . There was always a "but." As a former colleague of mine used to say, "Argue for your limitations and sure enough they are yours." Ed had been arguing for his limitations for a long time. We all do, without realizing it. "I would, but . . ." "The time isn't right," "I don't have enough money," "It's too soon (or too late)." We go through a litany of if-onlys, putting the perceived limit outside ourselves where we are powerless to do anything about it.

Ed had actually changed his circumstances, though. About three years earlier he had looked his perceived limitations in the eye and in effect said, "You will no longer stop me." He let go of all excuses, got a loan, and went back to school.

I'll never forget seeing all those A's on his first report card. I wept with pride and gratitude. But "now this." He had to begin paying off the loan and at the moment it looked bigger than his capacity to handle. He was reaching out to me, and I wanted to say just the right thing.

As a mother my instinct was to rush in and fix things for him, but I knew that if I did I would short-circuit his discovery of the greatness in himself. I knew that he would not grow faith in himself and, hopefully, in God if I fixed this one. I wanted him to believe in himself just as I believed in him. All I could muster to say at the time was, "I'll pray for you, Ed," but somehow that seemed to help him.

I thought about all the times I had felt that way—not up to what life was asking of me. How often the limitations I saw were born out of my fears of the unknown and of failure. I've counseled and prayed with so many people who believed that they could not handle what was being asked of them, who were afraid to make a change that seemed so necessary, who believed that the circumstances were beyond their capacities, who believed that the facts of their lives were the truth rather than opportunities to find the truth about the power of God within them and all around them. Yet every time we prayed together their hope was rekindled and their spirits brightened.

One prayer may not instantly transform a lifetime of believing in limitation, but each prayer is a drop of hope that dissolves some of the burden of our "I can't" beliefs.

The divine seed that dwells within us is always calling us to become all we can be. The difficulties, the perceived limitations, the challenges walk us up to the threshold of what we really believe about our God and ourselves.

Each time we face something that looks bigger than our known capacities, each time we face a difficulty, we face a choice point. Will we choose to dance with our fears or dance with our dreams? Will we put the creative power of our faith in the problem or in the possibility? Will we direct our thoughts toward the infinite resources of God or will we direct our thoughts to all of the limitations we can see and imagine?

After praying for the words that would somehow encourage him, I sent Ed an e-mail. I said, "I have had lots of thoughts since our conversation and wanted to share some of them with you in the hope that you might feel some new hope. I remember how terrified I was when your dad and I split. I had no money, no job, and two small children and myself to support. I felt panicky. I remember just trying to put one foot in front of another, praying for God to help and guide me all the time. I began to look for jobs and find baby-sitters. It was hard juggling work and being the mom I wanted to be to you and your sister, but we never starved and our bills were always paid—and I was always amazed.

"I came to believe that God was doing for me what I didn't know how to do for myself. I know this is true for you too, Ed. God will show you how to make that twenty thousand dollars, guiding you to the right and perfect people and opportunities. God will give you ideas about where and how to get business. You will be amazed. Just ask for God's help, willing to follow the ideas that come. A bigger life has been calling you for a long time. You have hopes and dreams and they are God-given. And God always matches the dream to the dreamer.

"When you said yes to going back to school for your degree after so many years of thinking about it, you were saying yes to a bigger life, a greater life, and, most of all, to God's call. God has a divine plan for your life that will use all of your gifts and talents and will also bring out talents you don't even know you have.

"Trust me on this, Ed. When you take on something that is bigger than you think you can handle and ask God to help, God helps more than you can even imagine right now. You start leading a blessed life—not without challenges, because that's the stuff that heroes are made of—but blessed with resources beyond what you would ever expect. So you have a loan that looks daunting. Put God to the test! Ask God for something bigger than you think you yourself can do—like getting the loan paid off this year. God will do it through you, if you will ask and follow the guidance that comes."

That is true for each of us. We can argue for our limitations, thereby putting our faith in them, or we can ask God for help, believing in God's limitlessness and its availability to us.

Ed had a discouragingly slow start in his new job, which paid on a commission-only basis. But he gave it his all, working diligently, putting in long hours. He had become willing to see his situation in a different way and had grown just a little bit of faith. The result? Two years later he has not only managed to keep up his monthly payments on his college loan and pay off the loan on his truck, but he has also been able to buy himself a beautiful gold Mercedes—used but in mint condition.

Every moment of every day God actually calls us to a bigger life through the moments when we are asked to love more than we think we are capable of or even want to; moments when we are asked to say the kind thing rather than the impatient, intolerant thing; moments when we are brought to the edge of all that we know and trust and asked to jump into the dark unknown. Each of us has been given the freedom to choose to practice principles that limit us or the spiritual principles that prosper us.

The old adage is true: If it is to be, it is up to me. Yet we are never alone and on our own. The Spirit of creativity that spawned the universe always seeks to create in and through us. The opulence of God forever woos us to partnership in the abundant life.

What Is Prosperity?

In his book *Spiritual Economics*, Eric Butterworth, bestselling author and founder of three powerful Unity ministries, said that "lack and limitation of any kind are aberrations in an opulent Universe." God is abundance itself—the infinite potential of everything we can imagine and more. This same God who abides at the center of our being could want no less for each of us. The key is to build an abundance consciousness—a way or trend of thinking that aligns in any given moment or circumstance with the abundance of God.

An abundance consciousness is one that has been purified of all beliefs that cannot "see" beyond lack and limitation. Butterworth also says "God is the ceaseless flow of substance, and no matter what the extent of the need, Universal substance can easily supply it. But there is one thing God cannot do. God cannot supply lack. This is because lack is a state of mind and the condition cannot be remedied until the state of mind is altered."

In his book *The Hidden Heart of the Cosmos*, cosmologist Brian Swimme, Ph.D., tells us that the native people of South America teach that to become human "one must make room in oneself for the immensities of the universe." Our God is a God of immensities and we as the offspring have the innate capacity to create a work of art with our lives using the palette of God's immensities—the abundance of every good thing that we can imagine and more.

The following eight spiritual principles, along with the prayers and practices designed specifically for them, will help you create an expanded abundance consciousness. As you work with them, pray the thought that you are cocreating with God the life you dream of. Call God in like a trusted, beloved friend who will gladly join you on this adventure.

Go slowly. This week you might want to try just one principle along with one practice. Then try another next week. Or do one per month. There really is no rush.

Eight Practices for Moving from Lack to Abundance

1. *Establish order.*

Divine order is the energy that creates clarity of purpose and intent, establishes right priorities, attracts synchronicity, and motivates right action. It is putting first things first—first the seed, then the sprout, then the ear of corn. We align ourselves with this miracle-working power by putting our priorities in order. This creates an opening for us to receive infinite blessings. The key is putting God first in our lives.

In Scripture we are promised that if we will put God first in our lives, all our needs will be met according to God's riches and beyond our highest flights of imagination. Putting God first means beginning each day in prayer, asking God to order our day, our thinking, and our actions according to His will. We ask in prayer what God's will is, and do what comes to us to do.

As you take steps to establish order by putting God first in your life, it is helpful as a reminder, reinforcement, and complement to do physical things. I started with a committed prayer practice, saying morning and night prayers on my knees, and grace before meals. Then I began to add physical components. I started with my dresser drawers, one at a time. I balanced my checkbook to the penny and did my monthly expense report regularly and consistently each month. Then I organized my closets, putting blouses in one area sorted by color. I did that for my skirts, slacks, and suits as well. Now when I look in my closet, I actually feel peace and joy. Strange as it may seem, I feel prosperous—a sense of spaciousness and abundance.

Expressing order is done in simple (but not necessarily easy) ways—attention and appreciation given to family and friends, giving your best at work each day. It can mean showing up on time for appointments, keeping your word, keeping your car clean. Find your own version of divine order and watch the miracles. But always the most important thing is to put God first, people second, and things third.

Affirmations:

I put God first in my life and God puts my life in order.

I order my day with God and God orders my way with good.

Prayer:

Dear God, I put my day in Your hands. I know that Your plan will be a good one and so I thank You now for opening the door to wonderful experiences, right direction, and a day of joy and fulfillment.

Practices:

- Put God first by starting each day with prayer, asking God to guide your thoughts and order your activities.

- Do one small order project a day—clean out a drawer or a closet.

- Reflect on your priorities in life. . . . What really are the three or four most important things in your life? (Are you willing to put God first?) How can you begin ordering your life by them? If your family is among the top four, how will you invest your time today in your family?

2. *Take God as your partner and employer.*

Taking God as your partner and employer frees you from feeling that your happiness and well-being are dependent on anyone or anything else. When we feel that way we tend to hold back, not giving what we are capable of and not being who we are capable of being. The result is that we feel frustrated and discontented—the antithesis of prosperous. But when God is our partner, we are freed to give our best and to more fully express our creativity, no matter what our coworkers or employer may be doing or not doing. The more you give your best, the bigger your best becomes and the greater your sense of fulfillment. Your consciousness expands to accommodate the greatness in you that always seeks fuller expression.

Taking God as your partner and employer helps you to live courageously, not letting your fears and insecurities stop you. You come to know that your true security comes from God, not from your job, your car, your home, or another person. When God is our partner, we are empowered to do what we fear, to follow our dreams, because we are strengthened by a higher power that cannot fail.

One way to partner with God is to write a covenant with God, promising to give your best, dedicating all that you do to God. God's part is to supply you with an abundance of all things necessary to live a successful, happy life. You write what you are willing to give and to receive from the infinite abundance of God.

I wrote my first covenant when I was without a job. I had just finished training for the ministry and was having difficulty finding placement in a church. I wrote: "I, Sharon Connors, dedicate myself and all that I do to You, God. I promise to give my best and seek to honor You. It is agreed that You will bless my work and my life in every good way." After that I became clear about what I wanted and needed to do and was able to find the perfect church for me. I have done a new covenant each year on New Year's Day and always feel energized, encouraged, empowered, and excited by it.

You can also partner with God each morning in your prayer time, asking that you be guided to fulfill God's goal for your day.

You might ask that God take your worries and stresses and help you give your best. One of the things I do each morning to partner with God is to get on my knees and say, "I consecrate and dedicate this day to You, Lord. Glorify Your name in me." Since I started this practice, I've noticed that my days have gone much better and things don't throw me the way they used to.

The other day my office manager asked me how I managed to stay calm when it seemed that our efforts were being thwarted and the delays endless. I told her that I had the best partner helping me—God! Without reminding myself that God is my partner, my attitude would have declined as the delays and difficulties grew. Then I would feel a sense of lack and limitation, impatience and intolerance—no sense of abundance to be found there. Reminding myself that God is my partner helps me relax, do my best, and let go of the rest.

Jesus said, "I came that you may have life and have it abundantly." The Divine in us is our partner and will show us the way to open the doors to the abundance that God is and bring it into our lives.

> *Affirmation: God is my partner and*
> *God never fails.*

Prayer:

>   Dear God, help me live courageously, following my
> dreams. Take my fear and help me move my feet.

>   Dear God, I dedicate myself, all that I am and all that I
> do, to You. I can't wait to see what exciting things we'll do
> together.

Practices:

* Write a partnership-with-God prayer, a covenant, and
  read it daily. Include what you are willing to give and

what God in turn will supply. Here's an example: "God, I take You to be my partner and employer. I dedicate the resources of my mind, my heart, and my hands to you, knowing that You supply me with all things necessary to live an abundant life." Take time to be still and pray before doing this.

- In your morning prayers, take God as your partner for the day, asking God to guide all of your choices and to help you think big rather than small.

- Remind yourself each day, especially in the midst of problems and difficulties, that you are working for God. Give your best for God.

3. *Forgive yourself and all others.*

I officiated at a funeral recently for an extraordinary man who, knowing that he was about to die of the cancer that was ravaging his body, had planned his service down to the last detail. He wanted it to be a celebration. He asked that as a part of his eulogy I say that he wanted people to know that he forgave everybody for everything and that forgiving everyone was the most important thing that he had ever done. He said it had set him free. Everyone could tell it had. The ceremony included a PowerPoint presentation with the significant people and events of his life—days in Hawaii on the golf course with his beloved wife, holidays with his children. There were flowers and candles everywhere and the service closed with his favorite rock-and-roll music. He was free indeed with the freedom of Spirit.

Unforgiveness is like a clamp on our prosperity. It blocks the arteries of life through which blessings flow. Holding resentments keeps us focused on what is not right and what is missing. Every time we entertain the ways we have been offended, we energize a sense of lack rather than abundance.

Prosperity is more than money and things. It is a condition in which our spirit is fed. Forgiveness feeds our spirit. Unforgiveness shrivels our spirit. Jesus talked more about forgiveness than almost anything else. He said that to be free indeed we needed not only to love those who love us, we needed to love our enemies. As my friend John did, we need to forgive everybody and everything.

Actually, our humanness has a terrible time with forgiveness. Our hearts are fragile without the fortification of Spirit. Holding on to resentments may keep us feeling defended against the hurts of life, but defenses also wall us off from experiencing true prosperity—freedom, peace, and joy.

When we pray for willingness to forgive—and that is all that is asked—we invoke the infinite abundance of divine love to dissolve the sludge of resentments and set us free to live fully and joyfully.

Affirmations:

The healing love of God now sets me free from all resentment and its causes and results.

I give my resentment to God and God gives me peace and joy.

Prayers:

Dear God, I am willing to forgive. Take my unwillingness.

Dear God, I am having a hard time forgiving right now. I am angry and hurt and want to get even. I feel trapped in my anger, Lord, and ask You to open the way for me to be free.

Practices:

- Close each day with prayer and reflection.

- Reflecting on the day, see if you feel any sense of separation from anybody. Has someone offended you? Did you make someone wrong? Gossip? Are you angry with anyone? Take a moment to send each one a kind thought and good wishes.

● Take time to see if you have judged yourself harshly or done something you regret or not done something that you wish you had done. With compassion for yourself, give those things to God and ask God to help you do better. Then let it all go in faith to the transforming love of God.

4. *Tithe*

Tithing, giving 10 percent of our income (or our time and talents) to the source of our spiritual nourishment, is an intentional way to put God first, which all spiritual traditions say is the first requirement for living a happy, fruitful life. Why? I believe it's because tithing brings up all of our fears and puts them in the crucible of our faith, and our faith has to expand to hold and transform them. Tithing seems to jar loose all of our well-dressed rationalizations for limiting ourselves and keeping our lives small.

It also challenges every belief we hold about who and what God is. We are forced in the process to look at where we really put our faith.

I'll never forget sitting in church on a sparkling Saturday in Florida, and hanging on the minister's every word as she spoke about prosperity. When she said that tithing was a spiritual law that contained within it the promise of my life being graced in the most wondrous ways, I listened with every bone in my body. This was new to me. In the church of my childhood, tithing was spoken of as an obligation, with heavy undertones of guilt. Now here was this woman explaining that tithing carried not an obligation but a promise of rich rewards.

She quoted Malachi 3:10 from the Old Testament: "Bring the full tithes into the storehouse, that there may be food in my house; and thereby put me to the test, says the Lord of hosts, if I will not open the windows of heaven for you and pour out an overflowing blessing." I was hooked.

I made a decision to try tithing based on that promise, exhilarated by the invitation to actually put God to the test. I was self-employed at the time, separated from my husband and living in an apartment that seemed to be beyond my means. I was never sure from one month to the next if I'd be able to pay my rent, let alone the other bills. I was filled with new hope at the thought of working with God to improve this situation.

I started the test by buying a spiral notebook that day. I would note every penny of income on the left side of the page. At the end of the week, I tallied up my income from sales and entered the amount. Then I took 10 percent of the total and put it on the right side and wrote the check to my church, the one in which I had heard about this new way of thinking about tithing.

Doing that each week scared me about as much as anything I had ever done. I monitored the development in my notebook carefully and with growing amazement over the following months as I noticed the increase in my income. Even more miraculous, all my bills were paid with ease and there always seemed to be money in my checkbook . . . significantly more than circumstances warranted. I also noticed that when I prayed, I felt a much greater sense of intimacy with God. God was becoming a trusted friend. My faith was expanding in every area. This life-transforming experience was one of the reasons I could write to my son years later with unequivocal faith that if he would ask God for help, God would help him find a way to do what looked impossible to him. I could stand in faith that God would prosper him beyond what he could imagine. And God has.

Since those days, I have taught prosperity classes every year, over twenty now, with a passion that comes from a life that has been turned around and incredibly blessed by the power of this spiritual practice.

Yet the tithing principle goes beyond giving a tenth of our income to the source of our spiritual nourishment. Tithing our time and talent is an integral part of the principle as well. As we give in service to God, receiving no direct financial remuneration, we find that time expands on our behalf and that our talents increase as well. Tithing our money increases our financial supply. Tithing time increases our supply of time. Tithing our talents increases our supply of talents.

Affirmations:

My tithe is my trust in God and God proves my trust with wonders and miracles.

I put God first with my time, talents, and treasures and God puts me where I am most richly rewarded.

Prayers:

God, I am putting my faith in You. Prove Yourself in my life.

Dear God, I am going to try this. I feel scared and unsure. Yet, I am excited about the possibilities. Steady my heart and prove my faith. Thank You. Thank You.

Dear God, as I look around, it is so easy to see Your opulence, to see the beauty and wonders of creation. I breathe in the thought that this very same opulence that I see outside of myself is also inside and is the potential of every good thing I can imagine. I offer myself and all that I am and hope to be to You, trusting that You will work in and through me to bless my life in every way and help me be a blessing to others. Thank You, God.

Tithing Practices:

- Begin with a percentage of your income that stretches your faith—perhaps 5 percent—and work your way up to 10 percent within the year.

- Find a place to be in service, giving your gifts and talents in the place you call your spiritual home or any other place that nurtures you spiritually.

- Have a mind-set of "How can I serve and contribute here?" wherever you are. Make whatever you do a prayerful investment.

- As you practice this tithing plan, notice daily any improvements in your life. Keep a journal and thank God for the good in each day. Get ready for miracles!

- Bless your bills as you pay them. Bless your paycheck as you cash it or deposit it.

5. Develop an attitude of gratitude.

Gratitude is one of the most powerful spiritual energies in the universe, so powerful that I have devoted the last chapter to exploring it. It is really a form of love, the very essence of creativity. When we are not grateful, we have fallen out of love with life. And when we have fallen out of love with life, we are no longer an open channel for the resources and blessings of God.

Expressing gratitude engages the resources of heaven and we become magnetic to blessings. Feeling and expressing gratitude aligns us with the universal cycle of giving and receiving in a way that keeps the avenues of our lives open to the flow of divine abundance. Gratitude is the great multiplier. If you want more love in your life, begin to give thanks for all the people in your life, each kindness done. If you want more rewarding work, begin to give thanks for the work you have. If you want more money, begin to give thanks for your current income.

The more you are grateful the more you will find good things happening in your days that you could never even have imagined. Beyond that, something happens in us that is quite extraordinary. Our confidence grows. Our gifts and talents grow and expand and we discover we have gifts that we didn't know we had. The more we give thanks for everything, even the challenges, the more enriched our lives become.

Bob had agreed to lead a project in the church. He and his wife loved the church and had always been great supporters. Fortuitously, Bob was not home one evening I called their home. Instead his wife, Leanne, and I had a crucial conversation. She said, "Bob is just the person for this project. He would do anything for the church, but you have to know one thing—he needs to be appreciated."

It is so easy to not only take the good in our lives for granted—the simple things like food, shelter, clothing, and work. It is just as easy to take the people in our lives for granted. We rush through our days focused on ourselves and fail to appreciate the people in our lives. No one can be appreciated too much. Gestures of gratitude are the most enriching gifts we can give. Both the giver and receiver are blessed.

Affirmations:

I count my blessings and my blessings multiply.

I give thanks to God and God's good pours into my life.

I keep my focus on giving and the good I receive is multiplied.

Prayers:

Dear God, give me a generous heart. Keep me grateful for all that I have and let me not be afraid to give. Let me remember to offer all that I do to You, giving the best that

I've got and trusting that Your rewards will quench my soul's true thirsts.

Dear God, help me to look at my world through eyes of gratitude. Keep my vision on the good that I have rather than on what I don't have. Let me count my blessings, not my problems. Grow in me a mind of abundance.

Practices: (See also Chapter 11)

- Taking nothing for granted, count your blessings today. Before going to bed, count every good thing that happened, every conversation that went well, each person that contributed to your life that day.

- Write a note of appreciation today to someone special in your life.

6. Do what you love and love what you do.

One evening en route to a friend's home for dinner, a huge billboard caught my attention. A four-letter word dominated the expanse—*Work*—and in bold lettering just below it the words *For the Fun of It*. Just five simple words that hold one of the secrets of abundant living.

When you feel a passion for what you do, the universe opens its storehouse of treasures to you. When you don't love what you do, every day feels like a burden. Your life force is actually dissipated and this generates an array of negative states of mind—resentment, competitiveness, self-centeredness, pessimism, judgment, blame, and insecurity.

If we do not love what we do, we have two choices. We can change what we do or change our attitude about what we are doing. Often the biggest challenge is getting clear about what you love. For this reason it is important to take time to regularly reflect on what you value, what you love to do, and what your gifts and talents are. You can do this through prayer.

En route to Dallas I sat next to a man who was a sales manager for Dell computers. He asked me about the book I was reading, *How to Find Your Mission in Life* by Richard N. Bolles. The title had attracted my attention, I told him, and then I read Bolles's belief about our primary mission in life: "To seek to stand hour by hour in the conscious presence of God, the One from whom your Mission is derived." After that, I knew I wanted to read the whole book. I shared the mission of my church with him: "To inspire and empower abundant living."

He answered, "I like that. I have one too, but I think mine might be too long." He pulled it up on his laptop, saying, "I researched other mission statements before I wrote my own." He scrolled through three or four of them, including Dell's. Then we read his. It was beautiful, containing a list of the primary focuses of his life: to be a good husband and father, to give his best at work, and to treat all people fairly. It was a full page. I asked, "Of all the things you've listed, what do you have the most passion about?" He answered, "Making a difference for God and helping people see God through me."

This is what happens when we do what we love and love what we do. Others see the Divine shining through us and are blessed and inspired for their own lives. As the Divine finds expanded expression through us, we can't help but feel prosperous. When we are doing what we love to do we feel a sparkling joy and it is true that joy is the surest sign of the presence of God. When we are doing what we love and loving what we do, we are unconquerable in the face of difficulties. They do not bring us down but fire us up.

Marianne wanted to go to a conference on spirituality in Kansas City but she didn't have the money. I told her what one of my spiritual mentors had suggested to me: "You don't have a money problem. You have an idea problem." I said, "I know there is a way for you to go." We prayed. That was in February; the conference was set for June. In April I received an e-mail saying that she had the money and was all registered and ready to go. Here's what she did: One of the things she most loves to do is make masks. She decided that she would offer a mask-making workshop at her church and, in addition, sponsor a raffle for eight masks that she had made. She wrote, "The masks people made were *faaaabulous!!!* I swear I had more fun than any of them. It was so great to give them the basics and watch their imagination take off." And she earned some money at it, to boot. This is what doing what you love can do. Everyone is blessed.

Affirmations:

I do what I love and I love what I do, and all my dreams come true.

I give my love to what I do and what I do blesses and prospers me and countless others.

Prayers:

Dear God, You know me better than I know myself. Help me see Your will and plan clearly. Light Your mission for me so that I can see and follow.

Dear God, help me love what I do. Help me look for the good, nurture the good, and be grateful for the opportunity, knowing that this attitude will open the door to rich blessings and new joy.

Dear God, let this discontent that I feel guide me into doing what truly brings me contentment and joy. I give thanks for this discontent knowing that in it is the birth of a greater life. Guide my thoughts and lead me where You need me.

Practices:

* In prayer, ask what God's mission for your life is. It will be simple and given to you in a way that you will understand.

- If you are discontented in what you are doing, begin asking in your prayer time for clarity on the discontent. Is it about a change of attitude or a change in what you are doing? Write what comes to you. Even in the discontent, ask for the strength to be a presence of joy for others.

- Make a commitment each day to be your best and give your best.

- Make a list of things that you love to do. Make sure that your day has a good balance of them included.

7. *Take loving, committed care of your spiritual, mental, emotional, and physical well-being.*

To feel and be truly prosperous, we need to be fit on all three levels of our being—spirit, soul, and body.

Taking care of spirit means establishing and committing to a spiritual practice. Without being spiritually fit, the stresses and demands of life constantly throw us. We become irritable, hypersensitive, and dissatisfied. It is easy, then, to fall into being a victim or victimizer, living in self-pity or self-righteousness.

In Scripture, Paul urges the people in Ephesus to stay strong in their spiritual practices, seeking to grow into the fullness of the divinity within them so that they would no longer be tossed to and fro by what life brings them. This is what spiritual fitness does for us. We become resilient.

Jean has had one setback after another in the four years that I've known her. When I met her she had just lost her husband of fifty years to cancer after being his caretaker for the past year. Within the year following his death she fell twice, first breaking her hip and then her wrist. The following year, there was another fall and more surgery and hospitalization. She was back at church after each of those setbacks, despite casts and canes. I'd tell her, "I don't know how you do it, Jean." And she would always say with a little smile, "Well, you just have to make the best of things and keep on." Her faith was unshakable and so was her commitment to her spiritual life.

Taking care of the soul may sound daunting because the soul is a mystery. It is our essence yet invisible to the naked eye. Yet it yearns to be known so that it can be free—so that we can be free. The soul is the storehouse of all that we have been and all that we can be. It is the fastidious recorder of every thought. It is the keeper of the flame of our unique gifts, talents, and mission.

Taking care of the soul is seeking to know its mysteries. What makes you happy? What makes you sad? What are you afraid of and why? Why do you react as you do? Soul fitness comes with studying ourselves. It means taking an inventory of our motives and what is behind them. It is suggested to people in twelve-step programs that they make a searching and fearless moral inventory of themselves, acknowledging their mistakes, their fears, and resentments. They are cleaning up their past so that they can start life fresh and free.

The soul thrives in optimism and generosity and shrivels in pessimism and parsimoniousness. We cannot know the abundance of God when grasping or withholding or when driven by unknown fears or soured by resentments. We cannot know the abundance of God by ignoring the yearnings for creative expression that live in the soul.

Without being in conversation with the soul and finding ways to delight in its need for love, beauty, balance, and integrity, we see limits everywhere rather than possibilities. Life is bland rather than flavorful.

A good workout for the soul is a regimen of practicing spiritual principles in our daily lives, being persistently grateful, inventorying our shortcomings and taking steps to change our ways, forgiving everything and everybody, fiercely living in the moment, passionately following our dreams, loving as if there were no tomorrow and living life as a daring adventure. Our experience of abundant living flourishes as we do this.

Taking care of the body means coming to appreciate that your body is the temple of the living God. It is a sacred vessel and deserves respect and loving care. A physical fitness plan that arises from this understanding means giving our body the best kind of care and nutrition. It means not only nourishing food and drink, but nutritious thoughts and emotions, as well. It means exercising our mind as well as our body.

I've watched so many elderly decline prematurely because they neglect their bodies and stop exercising their minds. They begin to isolate, lose interest in the things and people around them. When we don't take loving care of our body, it breaks down. We lose vitality and along with it enthusiasm. As the energies of our body dull, our whole outlook on life dulls.

I was on a flight to St. Louis recently, and after we reached cruising altitude the flight attendant announced, "Ladies and gentlemen, notice the young lady coming down the aisle right now. That is Stephanie, one of our flight attendants. She has been on the *Dating Game* four times now and not gotten a date. So gentlemen, please pass your cards to the center as she passes." People looked at one another quizzically and a few snickers could be heard as the smiling flight attendant whisked past. I could feel my energy shift.

On our descent, the flight attendant came back on the intercom to say, "Ladies and gentlemen, please remain seated until my husband, I mean the captain, has brought the plane to a complete stop. Those of you going on to Hawaii with us, please remain seated." (Remember, the plane was flying east to St. Louis.) Now people were laughing wholeheartedly. She brought the house down when she added, "We have someone very special on board with us today. He is celebrating his one hundredth birthday and this is his first, I mean second, flight. Please stop and say hi to our captain as you leave." A robust cheer swelled through the plane.

That young lady blessed and bettered the lives of over two

hundred people that morning. She was a blithe spirit, ministering to the people in her charge. The abundance of her heart spilled into the lives of each of us. As we walked off the plane I am confident that we each felt a greater sense of life abundant. I couldn't help but think that our delightful flight attendant must have been in all-around fit condition to be such a blessing to others.

This is why we pray. By ourselves, maintaining peak condition of spirit, soul, and body seems out of reach.

Affirmations:

I take loving care of myself and I am filled with the joy of Spirit.

I care for my spirit and my spirit soars.

I care for my soul and I am set free.

I honor my body and it blesses me with vitality.

Prayers:

Dear God, fill me with enthusiasm for caring for my spirit, soul, and body. Let it be a work of joy. Help me make right choices and take right action. Let Your vibrancy be my vibrancy; Your joy, my joy; Your life, my life. I am ready. Show me how.

Dear God, keep me awake to the needs of my spirit, my soul, and my body. Help me respond in loving ways. Help me to be a good steward of all that You have given me.

Practices:

- Take care of your spirit. Take time to be still with your God each morning this week. In your quiet time, breathe the light of God into every bone and muscle, every organ and cell, affirming that you are being renewed spirit, soul, and body.

- Take care of your soul. In prayer ask Spirit to reveal what needs to be healed in you and your life. What needs to be changed, released? Journal it. Work with a spiritual director or coach if needed—someone who will support the changes you are willing to make. Pray, asking for guidance for taking right action. Then act.

- Take care of your body. Begin to take notice of life-depleting thoughts and release them to God. Check to see if you have habits that are life depleting. Ask God for help in eliminating them—one day at a time, one habit at a time.

- Exercise mind and body some each day.

8. *Practice nonresistance.*

When I went into labor with my first child in the wee hours one morning in May, my water had already broken. The labor pains started slowly but quickly became tidal waves before my husband and I could get to the hospital. When we finally arrived the nurses rushed me into the labor room to be prepped, promising something to relieve the pain once we got to the delivery room. The pain was excruciating by then. The nurses and doctors repeated a phrase that took me through the delivery— "Breathe and push." I considered it my mantra. My baby boy was headed down the birth canal and I needed to help his birth by not resisting the contractions. You see, it is resistance itself in the form of contractions that moves the baby in the womb down the birth canal and into the world.

As with giving birth to babies, giving birth to the dreams of our hearts always involves some kind of resistance. The examples are all around us. The resistance of gravity turns a cloud of atoms into a galaxy. The resistance of air pressure lifts a plane into the air. When we engage the resistance rather than resist it, we open the way to making our dreams come true. Jesus Christ said, "Agree with your adversary quickly." Whether our adversary is a thought, a perception, a person, or a circumstance, until we acknowledge its right to exist and use it to move us forward, down the birth canal of what we are becoming, we stay stuck and fighting our way through life, exhausted and bitter. The more we disagree with our adversary, the bigger and more looming our adversary becomes. Difficult as it is to accept sometimes, obstacles are not meant to keep us outside the gates of abundance but rather to help us open those gates.

The more we fight difficult people or circumstances, the more it feels as though our life is not working. We rob ourselves of the gifts of abundance—peace and joy.

The more we say, "This isn't fair," "I don't deserve this," "This shouldn't be happening," the less prosperous we feel. We feel cheated. Once we accept our "adversary" as worthy, we open the way to birthing a new aspect of the greatness in us.

Without prayer the spiritual leap to using resistance to sculpt a life that is rich and meaningful is too difficult for most of us. Prayer helps us put on the cloak of willingness rather than the armor of defendedness. It helps us wear the gloves of surrender rather than carry the sword of combativeness.

And so we turn to God in prayer to help us accept what is, thus clearing the way for a miracle of new birth.

Affirmations:

> I give up the fight and God gives me the victory.

> I give the struggle to God and God gives me the gift of new life.

Prayers:

> Dear God, I don't like what is happening. I don't even like how I am feeling. I give You all my resistance, asking that You do something useful with it. Show me the Truth and what You would have me know and do.

Dear God, I've been feeling stretched and stressed, on a merry-go-round of demands and busyness. I give all of that to You now and pause to breathe deep of Your peace and plenty. I breathe in peace remembering that You are my resource and will provide all that I need in order to do what needs to be done by me. I claim Your peace and abundant resourcing now.

Practices:

- Stay awake to ways in which you resist a situation or person. Defending your position; needing to be right; endeavoring to change another's mind or behavior through arguing, manipulating, controlling; avoiding necessary conversations or courageous actions—in fact, any time we lose our sense of peace and well-being—it's a good time to look and see if we are being resistant and unaccepting. When you find yourself unaccepting or resistant, stop, take a deep breath, and pray, giving the situation to God, and think a good thought.

- Find a church that feels like home. Equanimity in the face of challenge will come easier when you are part of a praying community.

Closing Prayer:

Dear God, let these simple practices be my daily bread. Let them be like yeast in my life, nourishing to my spirit, soul, and body; flavoring my every endeavor; letting me be a blessing to all who know me.

Chapter 9
Surrender and Willingness:
Prayers That Open Heaven's Door

During prayer God lifts the veils and opens the gates of the invisible, so that His servant is standing in front of Him. The prayer creates a secret connection between the one praying and the One prayed to. Prayer is the threshold at the entrance of God's reality.
—MUHAMMAD

I am a pencil in the hand of God.
—MOTHER TERESA

Dear God, I surrender all the things that seem to cloud my thinking and my capacity to love and feel joy. I surrender all my plans and all that troubles me today to You, willing for Your will, trusting that it will bless me with heavenly experiences.

I began my wondering about heaven when I was four. My grandmother suddenly disappeared from our home and my life, and I was told that she went to heaven. "Will I see her again?" I asked. "Someday in heaven," came my mother's answer. I remember feeling scared, but I didn't know what else to ask.

Whenever we went to family wakes, I was invariably brought to the casket to offer a prayer and I would hear the same kind of thing: Aunt Fannie is in heaven now. Poor Uncle Jackie. He is finally at peace in heaven now with God.

The mystery was spun deeper and richer in my grade school catechism classes. Heaven was located in time and space—when I died God would decide if I could be there, and "there" was up there somewhere, beyond where I could see.

It was, I was told, God's dwelling place, and the angels, saints, and people who live impeccable lives were there also. I never heard what they did there or how they all felt except for one word—happy.

The whole thing produced a lot of anxiety for me, though, because I was never quite sure what it took to get in and I was always scared that I couldn't do enough anyway. When I got to high school I became an agnostic about heaven. None of what I had been taught rang true anymore, but I was scared anyway. I hungered and thirsted for a personal relationship with God in the here and now; I didn't want to wait until I died! I wondered what I could do to pull back the veil that separated me from God and my dwelling place on earth from God's dwelling place in heaven.

In the coming years, after one failed marriage and a debilitating second one, I began to believe that the God of my understanding had deserted me. In the course of my seeking I was led to a teaching that answered my questions about heaven in ways that satisfied my soul and offered a way out of the hell I was experiencing.

The life-changing spiritual awakening came on a Sunday morning in mid-summer. I heard as if for the first time, "Heaven is within you. It is a state of mind that you can create by your thoughts." How radical a thought that was then. I came to believe that heaven can be created no matter what the circumstances may be. I came to believe through experience that, as Scripture says, the kingdom of heaven truly is within us in full potential and we experience it or not according to our attitudes, thoughts, and perceptions.

If we can believe that God is not an anthropomorphic being out beyond the trillions of galaxies in our universe but is the very energy of creation, the very energy of love and life; if we can believe that God is the order in the universe that defies description yet operates always to create an increase of elegance and beauty of form and life; if we can believe that we are made in the image and likeness of God—then we can begin to grasp the intention of the Divine seeking to be manifested and increased in and through us. The enormity of potential, power, and purposefulness that resides in each of us is both profound and alarming.

Take a moment right now to reflect on what you believe about heaven. How do you imagine it? What do you believe it takes to get there? Is it earned? Have you ever had an experience that you would describe as heavenly?

Experiencing Heaven or Hell

I was preparing a series of Sunday talks on "heaven" recently, and I decided to ask family, friends, and congregants for their current thinking on the topic. One of my first queries was to Mike and Faith, my minister friends in California. Michael said,

"Heaven? It is like grace. You know it when you experience it, but how do you put it into words?" He added, "Let me give you an example." He launched into an amazing tale of surrender and willingness, of heaven and hell.

He began, "Faith and I had the most awful week. My car was stolen on Monday. Then Faith had three rings worth twenty-five thousand dollars stolen, too. One of them was her mother's diamond, which was given to Faith when her mother was killed. The other was her sister Hope's diamond, which had been given to Hope by her mother and then passed on to Faith when Hope died last year. The third one was one that I gave Faith."

He continued, "We had our carpets cleaned that week and the next day Faith discovered that the rings were missing. She called the company right away to report what she believed was a theft. The owner said that both men had left the company but gave her phone numbers to try. She called both of them and was pretty sure it was one of them, but of course he denied it. She told him if he would just bring the rings back that would be the end of it. He just swore that it wasn't him.

"By now Faith was sure it was. I told her, 'Let me call him and rough him up a little bit on the phone. You are being way too easy on him.' But she said, 'I need to forgive him' and wouldn't let me call. I was angry.

"One night I just couldn't sleep, thinking about it. I decided to try a Buddhist practice called *tonglen*. It's a kind of meditation. First you breathe in what is painful and unwanted with the willingness and desire that you and others be free of suffering. Then you breathe out relief of the pain and suffering, wishing happiness for yourself and others. Just that, over and over again, until you actually feel some relief. When I got up the next day, I was able to release the anger. That day at church, Faith asked the congregation to pray for the young man that he would have a healing so that he would never have to do this again."

As I listened I thought, what a powerful example of surrender and willingness. Michael was willing to surrender his rage and resentment toward the young man. He was willing to see things differently. He surrendered the way he wanted to handle it. Both he and Faith were even willing to surrender getting the rings back.

But the story was far from over. On Monday after the congregation had prayed for the young man's healing and after Michael had prayed for him and released his resentment, the young man—his name was Don—called Faith. He said that he had been haunted and unable to sleep since she'd first called him. He broke down crying, saying that he was so afraid he'd have to go back to prison if he admitted that he took the rings. He agreed to bring one of them back but said that he had already sold the other two.

Michael continued: "When he arrived, we prayed with him and I asked if he knew where the other rings were. He said yes but that it was too dangerous for me to go there. When I told him I'd take him there and pay to get the rings back, he agreed but told me that I'd have to stay in the car or neither of us would get out alive.

"You should have seen this place. People were living in their cars or broken-down trailers and cardboard huts. Don apologized that I would have to see this. He had me stop near this old car and he went and knocked on the window. A guy named Buck came out and walked over to us. He eyed me up and down suspiciously. Don told him, 'I've got to get those rings back. This is my uncle and he has money to buy them back.' Buck looked me over again and then walked back to his car.

"He came back with one ring, saying he had already sold the other one. I pulled a couple hundred dollars from my pocket and asked if he could get it back. He nodded and walked over to a trailer nearby and disappeared inside.

"Meanwhile, I am doing *tonglen* and Don is alternately saying, 'I am so afraid I'll go to hell' and praying for Jesus to help him. I said, 'Don, look around. This is hell. You've created this life with your choices.'

"Buck came back with the last ring. I handed him the money and we left.

"As we drove away, Don said, 'I've never felt like this before. I did the right thing, didn't I?' 'Yes, you did,' I told him. 'You risked going back to prison to set something right. This is heaven and you created it by doing the right thing.' Don continued, 'But I don't feel God. God has abandoned me.'

" 'Don, look,' I said, 'God hasn't abandoned you. This whole thing is no accident. Think about it. You steal a ring from a minister named Faith and take Hope's diamond. Think about how you feel now and how it all worked out.' "

Mike closed the story by saying, "If I hadn't been able to forgive him like Faith had, this never would have happened. We never would have gotten the rings back. There would have been no resurrection if Jesus hadn't said, 'Father, forgive them.' "

Surrender and willingness open the doors of heaven to such an indescribable sense of peace and joy that we can only say heaven is right here on earth. By surrendering all of our thinking about our difficulties, confusion, chaos, or misfortune into the infinite power of God, we make an opening for God's reality. We are entered by God's reality as a peace that passes all understanding, compassion that is boundless, and clarity of perception that allows right action.

Both Mike and Faith had surrendered their anger and resentment. They surrendered their attachment to the rings and to retribution. Both were willing to forgive. Both prayed for the offender. Both had surrendered the whole situation in prayer into the power and grace of God, letting go of having it turn out a certain way. Mike also surrendered his fear regarding going into a very dangerous situation with the young man to get the rings back. The young man surrendered his terror of going back to prison in order to do the right thing. Each one surrendered the lesser for the greater and was willing to stand in the unknown for the sake of a greater possibility—God's will—which is always better than anything that we can imagine or manipulate.

Startling as it may seem or impossible as it may appear in the midst of a difficulty, heaven is just a thought away. As we transform our consciousness to be suffused with the will of God, which is always and only some form of good, we begin to create a heavenly internal environment, which enables us to create a heavenly external environment.

Exploring the idea that heaven is a state of mind and a condition of the heart, we consider prayers of surrender and prayers of willingness, which effectively create the setting for heavenly conditions to be born in us. These two ways of praying also free us from states of mind and conditions of the heart that block us from experiencing heaven on earth.

As we come to the Divine in an attitude of surrender and willingness, little by little we clear the decks of our souls and our lives for God to do what God does—create an increase of good in all of its earthly forms.

Choosing Heaven Now

In *The Marriage of Heaven and Hell,* the mystical poet William Blake created a dialogue with the prophet Isaiah: "Then I asked: Does a firm persuasion that a thing is so make it so? He replied: All poets believe that it does, and in ages of imagination this firm persuasion removed mountains; but many are not capable of a firm persuasion of anything." Your firm persuasion that heaven is an experience that you can create by the power of your thoughts opens the door for you.

When I first heard about the principle and practice of surrender, it frightened me. I thought it would make me weak, a real wimp. My dad had taught us to fight for what we thought was right and for what we wanted. He considered giving up a sign of having no backbone. But what I discovered is that surrender is not the same as giving up and that the spiritual practice of surrender actually *develops* backbone.

As I began to experiment with turning little things over to God, I felt a kind of relief that I had never felt before. I'd say the Serenity Prayer when I found myself upset because my husband was being cranky and I wanted him to be cheerful. Or if there was someone I was having a hard time liking (or even tolerating), I'd say, "God, love her through me because right now I just can't." When I needed to say something I was afraid to say, I'd say something like, "I am really afraid and need Your help. I give You the fear. Help me say what needs to be said." It always worked (and still does). I began to trust my God more and myself more, too.

As you give up your will, expectations, and resistance to what is and give in to God's will in prayer, guidance will come and it will feel right. Once you have surrendered a situation to God, trust that a sign will come or that God will reveal in your heart the next right step. After surrendering, don't take your will back, though. It will try really hard to come back. You may feel it as impatience or fear of the unknown. Keep turning it all over to God and, as Scripture says, watch and pray.

There are so many things that we want to have control of that we are absolutely powerless to control. We are ceaselessly tempted to control the future, people's feelings and opinions, and undesirable circumstances—to say nothing of our proclivity to be right at all costs. I heard a wonderful perspective on this: Would you rather be right or be happy? Take your pick. Until hearing that I had never thought of what I was doing as pressing to be right. I thought of it as just trying to be understood. Time after time my husband and I would end up arguing as I tried to get him to see things my way and he would just as staunchly defend his own perspective. It was both of us wanting to be right, and while we each stood in our small circle of rightness, we were anything but happy.

Tom, a member of our church, was afraid that he was going to lose his job. His sales production was down and so was his heart. He came to me for counseling, hoping for clarity on what to do next. He had lost his passion for the work but was afraid to even look for another job since this one paid him well and he knew it cold. Each time we talked, he was anxious about his boss's next visit to town, which occurred once a month. He would ask things like, "What do you think I should plan for the week?" "What should I say if he wants me to travel more?" He spun in speculation about what his boss would say and how to respond.

Tom could speculate till the moon turned blue and he would still be powerless over what his boss said and did. If Tom could surrender his need to be in control and have everything about his boss figured out, he might be able to get in touch with what he really has a passion for and would love to do. If he could surrender his fear of change and financial insecurity, and become at least willing to make a change or see his situation differently, he would create an opening for divine guidance. He would create an opportunity for God's plan to be revealed to him.

Is there a situation in your life that you are struggling with or a situation that you are spinning in, trying to figure it out? Try surrendering it to God. Put it in God's hands and keep your focus on what is before you to do. If the situation returns, keep giving it back to God. Breathe deep of faith that God will reveal what needs to be revealed so that you can do what needs to be done.

Willingness is the partner of surrender. In the face of his greatest challenges, Jesus said, "I came not to do my will but the will of Him who sent me." "My food is to do the will of Him who sent me." When his followers asked him to teach them to pray, he gave them what we know as the Lord's Prayer. He suggested that they go off by themselves and in the quiet affirm that God's kingdom of good be manifest and that God's will be done in the earth of their lives. Jesus totally trusted God and so was entirely willing for God's will. He suggested that his disciples could pray their way into that same kind of trust. And you and I can too.

The Answer

When for a purpose I had prayed and prayed and prayed until my words seemed worn and bare with arduous use, and *I had knocked and asked and knocked and asked again, and all my fervor and persistence brought no hope, I paused to give my weary brain a rest and ceased my anxious human cry. In that still moment, after self had tried and failed, there came a glorious vision of God's power, and lo, my prayer was answered in that hour.*

—Lowell Fillmore

The more you experiment with willingness for God's will to be done, however unknown or inscrutable it may be in the moment of prayer, the more you will come to experience the brilliance of God's divine plan for your life, heaven in the earth of the very situation that vexes and disturbs you. You will discover that your willingness toward a divine response magnetizes the most amazing help and outcomes.

The Christmas season had begun and my friend Liz called heartbroken and panicky because her holiday plans had blown apart. Her family, including her adult children, were scattered around the country. If ever there was a time when she didn't want to be alone, it was Christmas. For years she had been spending the holiday with her son and daughter and their families in Chicago. But she and her daughter Sheila had had a terrible falling out when she was there over Thanksgiving, and now, though she already had her airline ticket, she didn't know whether to stay in town or go. The thought of not being with her family was fiercely painful. She told me, "I've prayed and prayed to do what's best and I think I need to stay here for Christmas. It's scary but it feels right too. Sheila and I have talked and healing has begun, but I am just feeling like I need to be at home."

Liz did decide to stay in town and told me later that she had one of the best, most beautiful, and peaceful holidays she has had in a long time. The most amazing things happened. "I wound up having two Christmas parties to attend with people I love. I got a call from a man that I hadn't heard from in months. He asked me to go dancing and, I swear, it was heaven on earth. I even had a date for New Year's Eve, and that hasn't happened in years!" God's will is always better than we can even imagine.

In the Lord's Prayer, Jesus acknowledges the critical importance of aligning our thoughts, words, and actions with God when he says, "hallowed be Thy name. Thy kingdom come, Thy will be done on earth as it is in heaven." We are praying that God's will take root and grow in the earth of our thoughts, words, and actions. We invoke it in the earth of our experiences. Imagine thinking, speaking, and acting from the mind of God.

Willingness is a state of mind that has let go of control and is open to God's will. Trust that God's will is always for good comes little by little; it grows each time we let go of our grip on having life show up our way and no other way. One of my friends once said, "Everything I have ever let go of has claw marks on it."

My friend Denise told me recently that she had finally become willing to attend Al-Anon. Her husband has been a problem drinker for most of their marriage and little by little she has lost her health and even her sense of herself in trying to control his drinking and the fallout that resulted from it. We have talked about how painful it has been for her for years, yet she was never willing to surrender her control and ask for help. She told me, "I am so tired. I finally decided to give Al-Anon a real try." I congratulated her. "I know that took a lot of courage. I am so happy you are getting help for yourself." She went on, "I have lost myself in this. I realized that I am not the same person as I was fifteen years ago. I don't know what happened to *me*. I am so glad I don't feel alone anymore."

All those years Denise had been praying for her husband to change rather than praying to see clearly God's will for her. Once she gave up the struggle and prayed for help for herself, there came the tiniest bit of willingness to try something different. She finally surrendered into asking for help for herself. "It's just like a huge weight has been lifted. I know I never have to go through this again by myself," she said.

When we are willing and surrender, God shows us a way out of the turmoil and into just what we need to find peace and joy.

When it became devastatingly clear that I was powerless over my husband and his behavior under the influence of alcohol, like Denise I began the practice of praying for willingness toward God's will. I finally had to admit that I had tried everything I knew to control his moods when he had been drinking and I was a dismal failure. The more I tried to control his drinking, behavior, and moods, the worse things got and the worse I got. I was losing my sense of reality as well as myself.

Surprising as it may seem, accepting powerlessness opens the door for divine wisdom to be revealed. You will be set free from obsessive worry and fear. With clarity, you are able to discern the will of God and feel the rhythms of divine guidance.

Our individual prayers of surrender and willingness toward God's will are more powerful than we can imagine to transform not only our own lives but also the life of the world. We are at a crossroads in our history, where violence, injustice, and fear are in epidemic proportions. Yet in the midst of this we find pockets of profound compassion, forgiveness, and peace. It is a classic struggle not so much between good and evil as between a new order of existence struggling to be born in the midst of tremendous resistance from the old ways of seeing things. We see resistance globally to the will of the Divine for peace on earth and a brotherhood/sisterhood of man. When we become the energy of peace that surrender and willingness create, we make a significant contribution to world peace.

The biography *Gandhi the Man* tells of Gandhi admitting that all during the early years of his marriage he had forcefully imposed his opinions and will on his wife, Kasturbai. There were years of conflict in which he insisted on her utter obedience to his wishes. Kasturbai resisted his attempts to dominate her and to make her conform to his image of a dutiful wife. In a moment of clarity, he saw that he had not been practicing the principles of love that he preached. He experienced a quantum shift in his perspective by surrendering his insistence on his "rights" as a husband and becoming willing to focus his efforts on his "responsibilities" as a husband. The shift created peace in Gandhi. It generated peace in his relationship with his wife. This realization informed and guided his whole philosophy of resolving conflict through practicing the principles of love. He discovered that the most effective thing he could do was to embody the change he wanted to see in others.

Our humanness would have us fight or run from difficult experiences. When we resist in this way, life becomes a struggle and we miss the opportunity to know the treasures of heaven—peace and joy in all of their beautiful and life-giving expressions. We also miss the opportunity to discover the miracles of God's power and love responding to us.

To experience the greatness of God in us, and to taste true freedom, we need to trust enough to make a space for God to act in us and the circumstances of our lives.

Praying Courageously

My daughter Jennifer called me sobbing when she found out she was pregnant. She and her husband already had two beautiful boys and if they were to have another child they were clear that they wanted a girl. They were told by Jennifer's doctor that the chance of their having a girl was extremely slim since her husband came from a family that birthed primarily males. They had decided not to have any more children and had been practicing birth control. Now she was pregnant again and she was beside herself. She was sure she was going to have another boy. I invited her to pray, considering that this might be God's will and that God could and would make everything right. I said, "I know God will help you with this, Jen. Ask God what it's all about."

When we talked a week later, Jen was a new person. She said, "Mom, I've been reading the Bible and praying each morning. I know that this baby must really want me to be his mother and John to be his father. This must be God's will and I know it's going to be okay. I don't know what I'll do about having my girl, but having three boys is going to be great." In her way, she was surrendering, turning all of her fears about the situation over to God. She had become willing to see it another way and through reaching out to a power greater than her fear, was able to see her pregnancy and the probability of having another boy as a blessing rather than a burden. Sure enough, nine months later she delivered a beautiful baby boy—a child who now delights her endlessly.

Our human will leans toward doing whatever it takes to have our own way and to feel safe and secure. Often it is at great cost to our soul. In prayers of surrender and willingness, we reach out to a power greater than ourselves, a power of infinite wisdom, life, and love, and trust that heaven's answer and solution is always better than our humanness could fathom and that in that answer we will find true safety and security.

Diana is the caretaker of her aging mother, who is in the early stages of Alzheimer's disease, and of her sister, who is schizophrenic. The difficulties of managing the lives of these two women has increased in the last few years. The other day when I saw her, she had reached the end of her resources. "I had to put my sister in a nursing home this week. She was so angry with me. Her husband is ill too and is angry and afraid because he doesn't know what to do without her. On top of that my mother is growing more distant and needy." Tears began to pour. "I just can't do it anymore," she said. "I am losing myself."

We prayed, affirming that it was safe for her to let go and let God—to breathe and rest in God and be replenished; to let go of feeling that the weight of it all was on her shoulders. After we prayed, she said, "I don't know what I would do without the spiritual teachings I've learned here. Having a place to come and be refilled and having people to pray with is the only way I can do this."

We don't have to depend on our own strength and wits to handle the difficulties that life brings. We have a power that is much greater than any difficulty to lean on and be resourced and replenished.

Each time we remember to let go of having to figure everything out and surrender the situation into the mind of God, answers come. The more we can do this the more firmly persuaded we become that God *is* the answer and that a conversation with God, in prayer, is the way out of the struggle as well as into the fulfillment of our dreams.

Diana's problem didn't go away but the sense of burden did—the sense of hopelessness and helplessness abated as she prayed it into the infinite resources of God.

Sometimes we'd like to be willing to surrender our ideas about the way things should be in our relationships or in emotionally loaded circumstances, but we just can't. We can't seem to surrender the anger about feeling betrayed, misrepresented, or misunderstood. We just can't let go of the desire to "fight for our rights." Take the case of Susan and Julie. They worked at the same mental health agency and, in fact, Julie had hired Susan and mentored her during the first year of Susan's employment. After a year and a half Susan took a job with another agency, but continued to seek Julie's advice on her casework.

Five months later, Julie discovered that Susan was after more than advice. Behind Julie's back, Susan had been wooing Julie's clients away. Julie was outraged at the betrayal. After having it out with Susan, Julie still could not let go of the deep resentment she felt. She wanted to be willing to surrender—to let go of her desire to get even. Julie had connections and could hurt Susan's reputation and business if she wanted, making sure she blocked the flow of referrals to her.

"I got on my knees and prayed to be willing to be willing," she said, and added, "I would tell myself that what is really mine can't be taken from me, but it sure felt like it was. Each day, as I prayed for God's help and guidance, I noticed that I became a little more willing. I guess I had to let the hurt heal some first. I asked others to pray for me, too. Little by little I was able to let it go and wish Susan well. I could never have done it without prayer."

Asking Others to Pray for You

Whenever you are troubled or perplexed or find yourself struggling to make something work, ask one or two good friends to pray with you for clarity, guidance, and faith— whatever would help you let go and know that all is well because God is in charge.

Scripture is filled with stories of the lives of people who met the fiercest kinds of challenges along the road to building the life they dreamed of. Job lost everything he had worked so hard for. His body was racked with pain. He felt punished by God, as we can so easily feel, mistakenly. Then, in a flash of brilliance, he began to reflect on the wonders of the universe wrought by the same God who created him. He began to reflect on the blessings in his own life. He understood for the first time both the transcendent (everywhere present) and immanent (the indwelling) power of God. He surrendered all the fear, pain, despair, and self-pity into the power and alchemy of God. The result? Scripture tells us that Job's lost relationships were restored to him. He was comforted and blessed. His days were exceedingly more blessed and prosperous than earlier in his life. As the doors of heaven opened to Job in his surrender, they can and will open to you.

Surrender Is Not the Same
as Giving Up

If we pray and pray for our heart's desire, for some experience that would be heaven to us, and our prayers do not seem to be answered, we often lose faith in ourselves and in our God. We give up in anger and disappointment. Giving up in this way is not surrender.

It is so often hard for us to believe that in the stark winters of our lives, when our fondest prayers seem to go unanswered, that spring stirs deep beneath the surface of all the barrenness we see. Even in the winters of our discontent, our confusion, our loneliness, and our discouragement, even in the as-yet unsatisfied yearnings and hungers of our souls, spring is poised to burst through the earth of our lives if only we will surrender, having faith that the right and perfect answer already exists in divine mind. Surrendering into God as the very creative principle of good makes room for heaven to respond. We make room for a miracle.

It is as William James said: "Prayer doesn't change God. Prayer changes us." When we make our thinking and feeling conform to the nature of heaven, we open the door of our lives to heavenly experiences.

> *In all situations of life the will of God comes to us not merely as an external dictate of impersonal law but above all as an interior invitation of personal love. We must learn to realize that the love of God seeks us in every situation and seeks our good.*
>
> —Thomas Merton

While vacationing in Utah, I went to a "star party" offered by the resort where I was staying. Bob Gibson, a professor of astronomy at the community college in St. George, Utah, was there to welcome us to the "greatest show on earth." Just the name of the class, "star party," tells volumes about Bob's love for his subject. Every one of us in the class had our own enthusiasm fired up by his. As he talked about how stars are formed from fire at the core, he said, "You are really all stars. You are made of the stuff that stars are made of." He helped us see that we are all capable of creating heaven right where we are if we stoke the fire of the Divine at our core. He said, "The fire at the core of the star gets stirred up and moves outside of itself and creates. It is so radically alive at the core." And so are you and I. Believe it or not, you are vitally alive with the energy that created an elegantly beautiful and ordered universe and each of us. This unfathomable creative energy is inherent to your being and is available to work its wonders through you—and will when you are surrendered and willing.

Practices for Surrender and Willingness

- Make a prayer list of your heart's desires. Love each one as a God-given desire. Put your list in a special container and place it on an altar in your home. If you don't have an altar, create one. I have one in my office on my bookshelf. As you place this "chalice" of your desires on the altar, say a prayer of surrender to God.

- The next step is to discipline your thoughts regarding your desires. When any of them come to mind, love them, feel the joy of living in them, bless them, and return them to God. Keep your faith and enthusiasm fired up, but don't try to figure out how, when, or if your desire will be fulfilled. Guidance will come. Just stay open and expectant.

- Create a treasure map of one of your desires and place it where you can look at it regularly, surrendering every thought save those of appreciation, love, and excitement. (A treasure map is a picture board of words and pictures that depict your desire. I have a 24 x 36-inch one in my office titled "Celebrate Living." I pasted pictures of all of my favorite things on it—my children and grandchildren, someone getting a massage on a beach in Hawaii, a balloon, a lusciously landscaped home—with words like *family, travel adventures, woohoo, pleasure, fun, dream vacation, miracles.*) Since making the treasure map, I have had more family time, planned a family reunion (a first), enjoyed two fabulous travel adventures to ski, and been blessed with amazing miracles.

* Stay awake to any sense of struggle in your life and surrender the situation to God, thanking God in advance for the right and perfect outcome. With negative emotions, embrace them rather than fight them, and then pray them, surrendering them to God.

Affirmations:

I surrender my will into God's will and God pours blessings into my life.

I am willing for God's will to manifest in every area of my life.

I am magnetic to heavenly experiences and they are magnetic to me.

My willingness makes room for miracles.

Prayers

Dear God, I surrender my will to You today. I put all my thoughts, words, and actions in Your hands, trusting that You will guide me in every way. I stay expectant of good. Let me see with Your vision, hear Your will, choose with Your wisdom, and act in Your love.

Loving Lord, anoint me today with a vision of hope that renews my spirit. Let me see clearly what You would have me do to make my dreams come true. I surrender all doubt, worry, and struggle to You and I pursue what brings me joy.

Dear God, come pour Your healing love in me and let it scour my heart to shining and do its perfect refining so that I can see clearly Your countenance there and reflect it out into my life. Show me how to measure my days in all the ways that nourish my soul and contribute to create heaven on earth. Give me the courage to open my arms wide to life and to everybody in it.

Lord, I surrender my obsessive worrying and insistence on a certain outcome to You. It's not easy, though, Lord. So help me keep my focus on trusting that You have a much better answer than I do. Teach me that my hope is in You and let me rest in thoughts of Your blessings and miracles unfolding now.

Dear God, I come this morning with just a little willingness to let You work out the answers to all my heart questions. Grow my willingness into confidence and happy anticipation that Your plan is more wonderful than I can even imagine. I am ready.

Dear God, I pray. Make me an instrument of your goodness and love today. When I feel lost, show me the way. When I feel unsure, give me Your confidence. When I don't know what to do or say, give me Your thoughts. Grant me Your wisdom in each decision, Your clarity, patience, and peace in every deliberation, and Your courage in every good purpose. As Your love and goodness seek me today, let me be found.

Chapter 10

Finding Your True Purpose:

Prayers for Fulfillment

Our purpose is to express our divine potential. This purpose gives joy and zest to living. When our eye is on the goal, we are not so easily perturbed. Purpose awakens new trains of thought; purpose directs these thoughts into new fields of achievement. Really to succeed we must have some great purpose in mind, some goal toward which we are working. But, above all we must purpose in our hearts to achieve spiritually.
—CHARLES FILLMORE

Again and again the sacred texts tell us that our life's purpose is to understand and develop the power of our spirit, power that is vital to our mental and physical well-being.
—CAROLINE MYSS

Most amazing God, amaze me today as You light my way into fulfilling Your purpose for my life. I believe that my most beautiful dreams began in You and that You have a plan for my life that is a good one. I lean on that promise now. Be my light when I feel lost, my hope when in doubt, my courage in any fear, and my fortress in any storm as I move in the direction that I think You are leading me. Saturate my senses with Your vision for my life. Help me remember that when I come to the edge of all the light I know, You will give me wings or lead me to solid ground as I step into the unknown.

Wayne and I met on a plane between Phoenix and San Diego. He used to play football for my beloved Chicago Bears, and for the length of the flight he regaled me with stories and Bible quotations that had given him hope in the midst of his professional difficulties. He told me that during practice he would face the notorious Dick Butkus across the scrimmage line and pray, "Lord, deliver me quickly." And God did.

Wayne no longer plays football. He facilitates and coordinates the building of hospitals and schools in Third World countries. He said, "My work is so fulfilling. I feel like I am serving God. I used to dream of making a difference for God and now I feel like I am. I love what I do." God matches the dream to the dreamer. The dreams you love are the dreams that are tailor-made for you.

The places, relationships, and circumstances in which we find ourselves are not the true givers of fulfillment or grantors of a sense of purpose that satisfies the soul's thirst. Rather, they are the matrix for our discovery of authentic fulfillment and a purpose that is bigger than we are—one that will engage and use all of our creative juices and all of our gifts and talents.

If we are prayerful, our dreams lead us to treasures that no money can buy. Relationships, careers, hobbies, vocations, and avocations are all the handmaidens, the footmen, of the soul's journey to fulfillment. When our mind and heart grasp the reality of the divine urge to greatness in us, then the circumstances of life take on a new and significant meaning. We begin to look for divine direction in everything. That is, except when we are not looking.

There is a beautiful description of God's presence in us as the creative energy that seeks expression and embodiment in and through us. The Apostle Paul writes in his second letter to the Corinthians: "For it is God who commanded light to shine out of darkness, who has shone in our hearts to give the light of the knowledge of the glory of God . . . and we have this treasure in earthen vessels that the excellence of the power may be of God and not of us."

There is in each person a divine treasure that includes unique gifts and talents. Our gifts and talents have life, substance, and intelligence, and if we will enter the daring discipline of discovery and pray for ways to bring them out of the darkness and into the light of expression, we will find true fulfillment. This is the purpose of our lives: to embody the divine treasures within us and bring them to the world in love. We have our own unique contribution to make to the family of man. The body of God that mankind is will not be as whole, healthy, and vibrant without our contributing to it through fulfilling ourselves.

The Journey to Fulfillment

I was a young mother living in suburbia with two beautiful children, a lovely home, and feeling restless, discontented, and empty often enough that one afternoon it finally got my attention. I was standing at my kitchen window, washing up the breakfast dishes and feeling like a caged bird. I felt a silent scream inside my heart. I felt powerless, not knowing what to do to quiet the scream. I looked out the window to a God out there somewhere and prayed, "God, help me. Show me what to do to be free."

Less than a year later, my husband and I were in divorce court and I was getting free—but not in a way I ever wanted or expected. "God, this is not what I wanted. I am scared. I am afraid that I won't be able to take care of the children and myself. Show me how to do this."

At the time, my cry felt like a prayer for survival rather than fulfillment. But now I know that was not true. It was the opening of a door in my heart to discover God's greater plan. It was a spiritual awakening. I began a spiritual quest that led me to places I never expected to go, doing things I had always wanted to do and thought I never could.

The journey to find true purpose, one that can contain all the ups and downs, the disappointments and discouragement, the drive and the passion, calls us all to the highest possible intentions for living and tests our faith to the max as well. If we default and just settle, we will never know true peace and joy. We will never experience the bliss of finding the greatness within us either.

In our quest for a life that is fulfilling in every aspect, we discover what true security is: we will know, in the midst of all the stresses that life brings, that God has a plan for our lives and it is a good one.

Ask yourself: "What is it that would create a fulfilling life and give meaning that transcends all the roles I play? What is it that makes my life worth living?" Take a deep breath and consider the directions your life has taken. Is there a thread that weaves together the choices you've made? Is there a talent or interest you were aware of early in your life that has directed your decisions? Regardless of others' opinions, what do you believe to be the purpose of your life? What do you hope for? What brings you joy? What do you believe you ought to do in your life? How do you believe you should live? If you continue going in the direction you are now headed, where might you end up? Your answers will point the way to finding a purpose worthy of your greatness.

In the book *Our Prayer,* Louis Evely says, "Prayer is not asking things of God, but receiving what he wants to give you; it is not being heard by God, but hearing God praying to you. . . ." So what does prayer really amount to? It amounts to paying attention to God praying in us, forgetting our needs, our rebellions, our hopes, consenting to God's unfolding his plans for us. Can you imagine that praying to God to have your deepest yearnings satisfied is, in fact, God praying in you?

As God seeks communion with us, our soul responds. In Scripture the Psalmist sings: "Our soul thirsts for the Lord; he is our help and shield and our heart is glad in him." "As a deer longs for flowing streams, so longs my soul for thee, O God." "My soul thirsts for God, for the living God." (Psalms 25, 33, 42) Our soul thrives and sparkles with vitality when we seek and follow God's purpose for our lives. That purpose is revealed through our noblest dreams, in what brings us joy and in what grows our spiritual character.

A Simple Meditation on Life Purpose

Imagine yourself in one of your favorite places in the whole world, sitting in anticipation. Be in this place with all of your inner senses.

See Jesus walk over and sit next to you. Ask him to reveal your life's purpose in a way that you can understand. Be still. Watch and pray. Something will come—a word, a phrase, a symbol that is clear to you.

As you search your heart and soul through prayer, and become clear about what you truly value, about what gives you joy, life, and vitality, you will come face-to-face with what God sent you into the world to do. You will discover the most fundamental purpose for your life. It will feel right in your heart and will be somehow related to a dream that has lived in you all your life that seemed impossible. Within this greater dream will be many other dreams that will require you to step out of the well-anchored boat of your life to fulfill.

Recalling all of your accomplishments up to now, remember the challenges, how your faith was tested, maybe how you wanted to give up. Remember the feeling of rightness, like a deeper inner peace, even though the road was difficult, even though those around did not agree with you. Most of all remember the exhilaration you felt when you crossed the finish line into fulfillment of your dream or goal.

Now as you become really still and dig deep to explore the dreams that still live in your heart, pray with the following truths. Keep them in your close-by memory as you make a commitment to yourself to take steps that move you in the direction of making your dreams—at least one of them—come true.

Four Truths for Realizing Your Dreams

God has a plan for our lives, but God needs our full collaboration to fulfill the plan.

Cosmologist Brian Swimme approaches the creative call with a wonderful question: "How can we participate in the Creativity of the universe profoundly? The Creativity of the universe is articulating its intelligence through us at the rate that we allow." It is through prayers of surrender and willingness that we render ourselves a hollow reed through which the Creativity of the universe can play its exquisite music.

God's good plan for each life lives in the depths of our soul just as the oak lives in the acorn. It lives in palpable readiness waiting for us to take it by the hand, to marry our creative energy to it through prayer.

We must be willing to live outside of our comfort zones to discover more about ourselves, our God, and life.

My friend Howard is successful by all the world's standards. He has three beautiful, bright children, a solid marriage, a lovely home, and he is very successful at what he does. He gives everything he's got to his calling as a minister, and because he does, he often enough feels stretched beyond what he feels capable of. I asked him recently what fulfills him. He said, "I'm still hunting for it and trying to create it. I have moments of feeling fulfilled. It's feeling like I'm making a difference in people's lives. It's loving relationships. It's being on purpose each day—moving in the direction of my goals and dreams, keeping my focus steady and not letting difficulties or inconveniences distract or dissuade me. And I'm always working at it."

Fulfillment doesn't come upon us once and for all. There are always new dreams to fulfill, new fields of creative expression to seed, fertilize, and harvest. A sense of fulfillment comes each time you stretch yourself beyond your current level to live more fully, love more lavishly, and express your infinite creativity in new and expanded ways that uncover more of God's treasures in you, bring you more joy, and bless the people whose lives you touch.

Fulfillment is paradoxical. It is both a magic moment in time— a moment of sweet intimacy, a moment of feeling deeply appreciated for our efforts, a twenty-year dream finally fulfilled, an ineffable contentment—and a lifelong pilgrimage.

As long as we are alive, there is more to discover about our divine potential, more of our God-given gifts and talents to bring to the world, more of our divine character to develop. When we make this the focus of our days and our endeavors, fulfillment follows as day follows night.

The treasure within us is the divine seed that shows its texture and colors through our fondest hopes and highest dreams. Developing a spiritual practice that nurtures you into the fullest expression of the divine seed that is uniquely imprinted in your soul is one of the best and most powerful gifts you can give to yourself and the world. The spiritual energy that comes from consistent, daily prayer time is cumulative in its capacity to clarify, strengthen, and fortify. In the presence of spiritual energy, fears lose their power.

We can turn setbacks into comebacks.

When Robert Schuller set out to build his dream, the Crystal Cathedral, people said it was impossible. But nothing was going to deter Schuller. He wanted a church big enough for his vision and so he engaged Philip Johnson, one of the top architects in the country. Johnson, along with his partner, John Burgee, came back to Schuller with a design for a matchless all-glass church, but it was going to cost millions. As Schuller, his staff of ministers, and his board sat around the conference table discussing the "impossibility" of raising the necessary funds, Schuller, an imposing figure at six foot six inches, rose from his chair. Silencing the murmurs of disbelief, he pounded his fist on the table and said from the power of his faith, "That church will be built." Then, addressing the architect, he said, "Philip, I don't have the millions of dollars. I don't even have one million dollars. Philip, I don't have any money to build that church, but I will." And he did.

With God, no mountain is too high to keep you from climbing it. No obstacle is too awesome to keep you from overcoming it. No goal is too great to keep you from reaching it. No problem is too difficult to keep you from solving it. No adversary is too powerful to keep you from conquering it. No burden is too heavy to keep you from bearing it. No aspiration is too noble to keep you from attaining it.

—William Arthur Ward

The same can be true for you. The dreams that God has planted in your heart are the ones that often look impossible, but they are not. If they excite you just to think about them but scare you by their largeness, they are probably from God. Remember: What God calls you to do, God equips you to do. Your most impossible dreams can be built if you will partner with God and stay faithful to the principles of spiritual due diligence. This means believing, as Jesus said, "without a doubt," even when there is no sign that your dream is coming into being. It means that you keep praying for the next right step and taking it, though you may not be able to see where that step is leading you. It means feeling the fear and doing it anyway, even when you don't think you can do what needs to be done, trusting that God will guide you and equip you. It means giving your best right where you are, even when you don't want to. It means being a good steward of all that God has put in your hands—your spirit, soul, and body, your time and your talents, your family and friends and all of your possessions. It means using the obstacles to grow your spirit and move you forward. It means living as if the miracle was accomplished—until it is.

Whenever you endeavor to do the things that give your life meaning, when you go after your dreams, you can count on meeting with obstacles. They are a part of the creative process—in fact, they are caused by the friction of forward motion, by creative activity. But it is in praying for help and digging deep inside ourselves in the face of the obstacles, delays, disappointments, losses, and betrayals of life that we find the inner resources to transform them into something useful. And each time we meet the tests that chart the course of our spiritual evolution with prayer, and the courageous action that Spirit inevitably suggests, the greatness in us is grown.

Commitment magnetizes synchronicity and unforeseen help.

On my computer monitor, I keep W. N. Murray's much-quoted description of the power and magic of commitment. It always encourages me when I think about giving up:

Until one is committed, there is always hesitancy, the chance to draw back, always ineffectiveness. Concerning all acts of initiative (and creation), there is one elementary truth, the ignorance of which kills countless ideas and splendid plans: the moment one definitely commits oneself, then Providence moves too. All sorts of things occur to help one that would never otherwise have occurred. A whole stream of events issues from the decision, raising in one's favor all manner of unforeseen incidents and meetings and material assistance, which no man could have dreamt would have come his way.

It is important to remember that this kind of grace *follows* our heart commitment and taking action. Providence moves after we have taken steps in the direction of our dream—not before. We desperately desire help before we take a leap of faith, before we walk through the fear, before we handle the difficulty. But spiritual power is not developed in that way any more than physical muscles are built before we work out. Physical fitness comes as a result of lifting weights beyond what we think we can. It comes from *completing* an aerobic workout, not thinking about it. Our endurance and power are built only as we remain faithful to the workout. The guarantee is there before we begin, but we must begin.

Doing What You Love

From the time Ben started school, his parents dreaded the approach of fall each year. The call would invariably come. "Ben is a delight but he doesn't pay attention. If only he would pay attention, he could keep up." Ben was not interested in paying attention even if he could. His parents were baffled. They watched Ben, even at a young age, take his toys apart with great precision and then put them back together again—usually. They believed in his potential even as they watched him struggle in school, unable to access the potential that they knew was there.

When Ben was told that he would have to repeat his junior year in high school, he threw in the towel. He said, "I wished all through school that someone would teach me what I wanted to learn. When I dropped out of high school, my parents signed me up for the Outward Bound program. Something happened there. I discovered my love for the ocean and being in the water. Afterward I signed up for a scuba diving class and it all began to come together for me. My dad had always told me that if I found something that I love to do, I'd never 'work' a day in my life. I knew I had found it."

Ben began to dream, wondering how he could make a life and a living out of this thing that was nurturing his spirit. He was ready and willing to commit. Synchronistically, the magazine on scuba diving that he had ordered arrived. He had ordered it with no thought except that he wanted to know more about diving. As he thumbed through it, he discovered that there were six schools in the country where he could earn a degree in marine technology. "I knew this was my answer. My dad and I went to visit the school in Santa Barbara, California, and I knew I was home. I began teaching scuba, but after a while I felt restless again. Something was missing for me because I couldn't explain the beauty I saw in the silence of that underwater world.

"Then I saw an ad in the newspaper for a workshop in underwater photography and something clicked. The workshop was being given by the premier underwater photography experts in the world and they hadn't had an appearance in the States in thirty-five years. I didn't know why, but I knew I had to be at that workshop."

Ben went to the workshop and whole new worlds opened to him. He has now become an expert and sought-after underwater photographer himself. He's been asked to appear in motion pictures. He has already at the age of twenty-seven had his photographs published in numerous magazines. He has traveled around the world on underwater photography projects. And new opportunities keep knocking at his door. After his own persistent prayer and that of his parents, he did find something he loved and committed himself to it. And, as he tells it, he doesn't "work" a day in his life.

God has a plan for your life that is exquisitely good and profoundly meaningful. You can pray your way into the fulfillment of that plan.

⭐ 🍃

Your Quest Changes You

Beyond all of our fears and insecurities, beyond all of our angers and neediness, there is greatness in us awaiting our discovery and loving attention. God Who began a good work in you will be faithful to complete it—if you will only say yes and dare to take the steps to prove the promises.

Author Gregg Braden, an earth-science expert and guide to spiritual sites around the world, said this at a recent conference titled "Living in the Mind of God": "The blueprint of all of life exists in the quantum field." That is true for the dreams that speak of what we most love and value. They exist already in the quantum field, in the mind of God, awaiting our committed action that they might come to life in our life. Each step toward making this so is a piece of our true fulfillment. For this purpose we were born.

⭐ 🍃

Meditation

Close your eyes and take a deep, long, full breath, letting it fill your whole being. Breathe into the silence deep inside where the noise of life and thought fades. Breathe deeply and reflect on the truth that God planted seeds in your heart that were meant to become the brilliantly beautiful flowers of your dreams. Give one of your dreams life in your imagination. Look at it lovingly and gratefully. Then silently ask unto God, "What is my next step?" Be still, watch and pray and listen. Make a commitment to do whatever comes to you to do.

Practices

- **Pray seeking clarity** on what brings you joy, what you love to do, and what you most value. Write these things down, and then look at them each day in your prayer time. Pray for guidance on the next right steps. Take the actions that you are guided to take.

- **What are your three biggest, greatest dreams?** Write them down and read them regularly. Make a treasure map of them.

- **Gather a group of prayer partners** and begin to support one another in making dreams come true.

- **Practice building your capacity for commitment** with small, short-term commitments. Commitment builds power.

Affirmations:

I give my best and God does the rest.

God has a plan for my life, and it is fruitful, fabulous, and fulfilling.

God began a good work in me and will see it to completion.

Prayers

Dear God, amplify the sound of Your purpose in me; orchestrate my life to fulfill Your plan; enlarge my heart to encompass the fulfillment of Your presence and power living in and through me; let me be in service always to a larger cause than my own.

Most gracious Lord, Whose awesome plan for my life exceeds my greatest longings; Whose inexhaustible supply would provide for my every good desire; whose unerring wisdom would guide my every step into fulfilling my fondest hopes and highest dreams; and whose electrifying love yearns to light my heart and life in megawatts, come now with Your love, substance, and wisdom to move the fulfillment of Your plan for my life forward. I am ready and willing.

Lord of light, Whose dazzling brilliance seeks to dispel all darkness, shine Your shimmering love light in my heart today. From the point of light within Your mind, enlighten my mind. From the point of love within Your heart, let love guide my thoughts and plans and steps. From the center of my being where Your will is planted, let Your purpose be known to me now.

Dear God, I rejoice in this day, freely accepting the blessings that flow from Your allness into my life. This very day I accept my health, my joy, my abundance. If I sing, You are the music, and I am grateful. If my life has meaning, dear God, You are the meaning given. You set my spirit free; You are the light by which I see. Let me be Your light in the world today.

Chapter 11

Creating Miracles:

Prayers of Gratitude and Praise

The grateful heart is a dynamic key to personal prosperity. As you feel grateful you become attractive, not only in your beauty and radiance but in your relationship with people. More importantly, you release a vital energy that draws to you opportunities, employment, and a secure flow of substance.
—ERIC BUTTERWORTH

God of dazzling abundance and infinite generosity and goodness, create in me a grateful heart, one that trusts in the beautiful possibilities for my life even when I can't see them. Create in me a big heart so that I can appreciate all the good that fills my days. Create in me a confident spirit, confident enough to give thanks for everything, the difficulties that grow me, the blessings that await me, as well as all the little things that I tend to take for granted. And thank You for all of the blessings that this day holds.

My niece, Erin, was a bright, gregarious, and adorable child. She had everything going for her—a good home, good family, promising future. And there was never a doubt that my brother and sister-in-law loved her deeply. Then in her freshman year of high school things began to change. At first it was little things—slipping grades, notes from the teachers about homework not being done. Within a year things worsened dramatically. She started to stay out past curfew, argue with her parents, cut classes, and isolate from the family.

By the time Erin was a junior, her drinking and drug use had taken her down many dark roads. Whenever I talked with my sister-in-law, Joyce, she would have a new horror story. Joyce talked, too, about how her prayer life was deepening and expanding in the face of all this. Prayer became her constant companion. "I've asked everyone I know to pray with me for a turnaround in Erin, even my La Leche League friends," she said.

But a turnaround was looking more impossible every day. By her senior year, Erin was having brushes with the police, staying out all night, and losing interest in everything save partying with her friends. My brother and sister-in-law felt utterly powerless, but even in their darkest moments, when their prayers seemed fruitless, their love for Erin kept their hope alive and their prayers constant.

Miraculously, a turnaround did come. The summer after her senior year in high school, her father (my brother, Jim) took the family to Ireland to trace the family roots.

Something happened inside Erin on that trip. She experienced a total shift, a sudden flowering, I believe, of the years of prayer. It was what some call a spiritual awakening or a transformation of consciousness. As she tells it, in a moment of clarity she began to feel a deep sense of gratitude for all that her parents were doing for her, for their unfailing, though trodden-on, love for her. It was as if her whole life flashed before her and as it did, a profound sense of gratitude welled up in her heart. She saw the countless times she had been spared from disaster; the times she had hurt her parents and yet no matter what she did they never stopped loving her. She recalled with gratitude the many times her sister and brother had made excuses for her and tried to help her no matter how callous she had been.

Erin came home a new person. She asked for her parents' forgiveness and told them that she wanted to be baptized and start a new life. That weekend, prompted by her pastor, she told her story at her church to over a hundred teenagers. Joyce said, "She was poised and clear as she talked to them about how the power of God, the love of her family, and all the prayer that had been said for her had opened her heart to God and changed her. She told them that she was starting all over with her life and asked for their prayers."

She did begin a new life. She went on to college, studied abroad, and graduated with a degree in international relations. This is the miracle of gratitude.

Becoming Magnetic to Miracles

Of all the spiritual practices that I've known and tried, the practice of counting my blessings—taking nothing for granted, of giving praise and thanks to God for them, has been the most life-changing and deeply rewarding one. It hasn't seemed to matter how negative my state of mind has been; prayers of gratitude always turn it around. And I know that it will be so for you. When you are grateful, you are entranced by the fullness of God's love and the eyes of your heart are opened to the grace and goodness that is all around you and in you. You are able to see clearly the infinite possibilities instead of all the obstacles that stand in your way. When you are grateful to God, you say yes to God's eternal invitation to come dance in the field of miracles.

Gratitude magnetizes good into our lives. Earlier in the book I spoke of the alchemy of prayer. It changes energy as well as the very nature of our thoughts and emotions. Prayers of gratitude to God are a form of love, the highest vibration, power, and energy in the universe. Call it what you like, when the energy of gratitude shows up, things and people change for the better.

When I was growing up, I was always praying for miracles—the impossible dreams of my heart. They always seemed to happen for other people, though, and I wondered what these other people knew about praying that I didn't. Having found myself feeling powerless so often, my great desire for God's help in my life led me to pursue understanding the nature of miracles and how they happen. All the paths led to gratitude.

Jesus Christ's ministry was all about miracles, turning people and circumstances around, doing what seemed impossible. Referring to the miracles he worked, he said, "Most assuredly I say to you, he who believes in me, the works that I do he will do also and greater works than these he will do. . . ." The book *A Course in Miracles* suggests, "This is a course in miracles. It is a required course. Only the time you take it is optional . . . miracles occur naturally as expressions of love." We are invited by the very yearning of our soul to partner with the creative energy of the universe, ever stepping beyond all of the comfort zones of what we already know to explore the depths and breadths and heights of all possibility. And gratitude is essential to being a miracle worker.

Gratitude is a universal spiritual law. It works through one of the basic principles you read about in Chapter 1, the law of mind action. It works like this: The more you are grateful, the more the creative force of the universe gives you to be grateful for. It is guaranteed—because the law never fails.

The universe is reciprocal. That means, in this case, that when you give thanks, you engage the gratuitous goodness and graciousness of God. Before the miracles of the multiplication of the loaves and fish and the raising of Lazarus from the dead, Jesus gave thanks. In the midst of daily challenges to his integrity, his work, and his body, he gave thanks to God. In Paul's letter to his followers in Thessalonica regarding the relentless difficulties they experienced, he urged them to trust that just the other side of their current difficulty was a miracle. He told them to "rejoice always, pray constantly, and give thanks in all circumstances," promising them that they would cross the frontiers of their faith and be embraced by a miracle.

There are four transformative and miracle-producing practices of gratitude that will immerse you in a great adventure in prayer and minister to you in deeply healing ways.

The Four Ways of Gratitude

1. *Give thanks and praise for what you have rather than complaining about what you lack.*

2. *Give thanks for the difficulties and challenges you face.*

3. *Give thanks in advance for the good you seek.*

4. *Give thanks for belonging in the world, to the family of man and to God.*

✼ ✼

Give Thanks and Praise
for What You Have Rather Than
Complaining About What You Lack

This can really be a challenge to our way of seeing the world. Our humanness urges us to see what is missing, to complain and bemoan what is wrong in our lives. The truth is that this viewpoint only gets us more of the same.

Take the story of Jesus feeding the multitudes near the Sea of Galilee. He had just received the devastating news that his beloved friend John had been killed. As Matthew tells the story, Jesus withdrew when he heard this to be alone in prayer. Meanwhile, hearing that he was in the area, thousands had gathered—the way we do for a concert. People came from all around to be inspired and healed. When Jesus came ashore after his time alone, we are told that he was moved with compassion and spent the day healing the sick. As the day grew into evening, the disciples urged Jesus to send the crowds away to get something to eat. Jesus instead suggested that the disciples offer them food. They were incredulous, saying, "We have only five loaves here and two fish." Now, here comes the astounding miracle of multiplication. Jesus said, "Bring them here to me." Imagine the disciples' bewilderment. When the loaves and fish were brought, Jesus did not look at the meagerness of the supply relative to the huge need. He looked up to heaven—to the possibility—giving thanks for what he had, in utter faith that it was enough. He didn't say, "This won't work" or "This doesn't begin to be enough." He blessed what he had, and what he had became more than enough. And the same kind of miracle can happen for you when you give thanks for what you have, no matter how inadequate it appears to be.

My friend Tina worked as a solderer in a Detroit auto plant and hated it with a passion. "I didn't like anything about it," she said, "and everyone around me knew it. I'd complain to anyone who would listen." She would pray for something better while at the same time affirming day after day how dissatisfied she was with the job she had. As a result, she was getting nowhere except more dissatisfied.

Then a friend invited her to a workshop on prosperity given at the friend's church. That evening she heard about the power of giving thanks for what she had instead of complaining about it and lamenting what she lacked. With new hope and plenty of skepticism, she began to thank God for her job. She told me, "Some days I would almost choke on those words, but I did begin to notice that I wasn't dreading going to work anymore and that I actually wanted to give my best. Before long I was a top performer and even got an award."

It was not by accident that barely a year after she began to give thanks for the job she had that a miracle happened, an opportunity that was greater than she had ever imagined. Her church, the one where she had heard about giving thanks for what she had, gave her a scholarship plus expenses to go to school to study for the ministry. This dream had lived quietly in her heart for a very long time, hidden in the shadow of impossibility. If you will try this with anything in your life that seems inadequate or lacking, you will experience a miracle of the multiplication of what feeds your hungers.

My friend John is a man with the Midas touch. Everything he touches in his work turns to gold. He has generated astonishing levels of income starting with nothing. He and his family live in a palatial home and drive big cars and have the best of everything. Except John doesn't have peace of mind. He lives in a constant state of stress. Rather than feeling grateful for the extraordinary abundance he has, he lives in fear that it won't be enough and that it won't last.

But I promise you that if you will adventure into giving thanks for what you have, even when your natural tendency may be to see it as not enough or to fear that it won't be enough or that you will lose it, you will open the door for more good to come into your life and to a peace of mind that becomes unshakable.

Give Thanks for the Difficulties and Challenges You Face

Take a deep breath on this one. The second adventure in gratitude prayers is probably the most demanding. Giving thanks for difficulties and challenges, ever holding the perspective that God is in the midst of the challenge as a potential good, is so alien to the human mind. But once you try this courageous prayer you will feel encouraged because it gives you hope and lifts your spirits.

Charles Fillmore, cofounder of Unity, suggested that we "pronounce every experience good and of God and by that mental attitude, we will call forth only the good. What seemed error will disappear and only good will remain."

Calling Forth the Good

Try this now with a challenge you face: Hold a prayerful thought that God is in the midst of it with a blessing. Begin to give thanks for the blessing and for the good that will come from this. Notice how you feel. Your whole being will be lifted, including your biochemistry.

Not long ago I attended a benefit for the Breast Cancer Fund in San Francisco. The presenters were all women who, out of gratitude for healing, wanted to share what they had learned on their journey. One of the women—we'll call her Mary Beth—

spoke about being grateful for the cancer itself. She said it brought her out of isolation and made her face things that she was afraid of. It moved her to reach out for help and support, repeatedly calling her to do courageous things. She became willing to seek a blessing in the adversity. Another woman, Julie, said that having cancer called her to courageously assess everything about her life. She said, "For the first time I looked at how to live my life from my pleasure. I made a commitment to myself to do only what is irresistible."

The Spanish poet Antonio Machado speaks to this kind of gratitude:

> *Last night, as I was sleeping*
> *I dreamt—marvelous error!—*
> *That I had a beehive*
> *Here inside my heart.*
> *And the golden bees*
> *Were making white combs*
> *And sweet honey*
> *From my old failures.*

Machado's poem suggests that even as we look at our difficulties, if we will pray a prayer of gratitude in faith that the transforming power of God is bringing something sweet to the palate of our heart, we will, without fail, find that the circumstance is transformed into a blessing.

Give Thanks in Advance for the Good You Seek

In all of Jesus' healing miracles, he "saw" the wholeness in the person before it was visible to the human eye. He saw it in the midst of the illness, disease, or debilitating condition. Recalling Jesus' feeding of the five thousand–plus with only a few loaves and fish, we read that he gave thanks *in advance* for having enough. He didn't wait until he saw it. He gave thanks before what he needed appeared. He saw the desired outcome done in his mind and gave thanks. In his mind he saw plenty right in the midst of what was an obvious lack.

If you will begin to give thanks now for the good you desire, as if you were already living in the answer to your prayers, you will begin to magnetize that good into your life. You will be guided to take the next right steps toward the miracle you seek.

We find another teaching example in the scriptural story of how Jacob healed the relationship with his brother.

Jacob, driven by his ambition for money and power, had betrayed his older brother, Esau, when they were young men. They had not spoken since. Jacob went to a distant land, where he amassed great wealth and had many children. But he always believed that if Esau ever tracked him down, he would kill Jacob on the spot.

Years later Jacob realized that he could not live in peace estranged as he was from his brother and in fear of his retaliation against his family as well as himself. And he decided to risk his life and a major portion of his wealth to seek his brother's forgiveness. He prayed for guidance and protection and moved his feet—to the very border of the land where Esau lived.

One night as Jacob waited in fear to meet his brother, he was overcome by a man who wrestled with him. They wrestled through the night, as we often do when we are afraid to do something we know we must do. Finally, the man realized that he was not going to overpower Jacob, and said, "Let me go, for the day breaks." Jacob, as exhausted as he must have been, responded, "I will not let You go until You bless me."

The very next morning, Esau came to Jacob and embraced him, and as Scripture tells us, "they wept."

Jacob believed in his miracle before he saw it and refused to give up or give in until he experienced its blessing. His persistence in believing and acting on his belief brought it about. The man Jacob wrestled with was none other than an angel, the Spirit of the Divine at the center of his being, who challenged him to be more than he thought he could be. The angel not only blessed Jacob but gave him a new name, Israel, for his willingness to enter into the creative struggle to birth the fullness and the stature of the Divine in him.

If we will grapple, as Jacob did, with all of the "angels" that challenge our faith and our self-formed identity, giving thanks in advance for the miracle embedded in the challenge, we will be blessed and increase in wisdom and stature. Jacob said, "I have seen God face-to-face and my life is preserved." You and I will actually experience God as well and feel a new and expanded sense of aliveness and efficacy. We will experience the exuberance of authentic power.

Give Thanks for Belonging in the World, to the Family of Man, and to God

The fourth, perhaps more subtle, way of adventuring in prayers of gratitude and praise is to say yes to belonging in all of its many unifying forms. It is the realization of who we really are as beings made in the very image and likeness of God and the astounding implications of that. In that realization, we know to the core that we belong to God and to one another and to all of life. This experience of unity transforms everything. We realize that we hold the key to living the life we dream of, that truly all things are possible to us.

Giving thanks for belonging to God, to others, and to all of life is the foundation for creating peace on earth—and true peace in our own lives. Saying yes to belonging is about giving thanks, by appreciating in thought, word, and deed our similarities *and* our differences. It is about a way of seeing one another that makes us brothers and sisters, that joins us rather than separates us. In appreciating our fundamental oneness, we heal feelings of isolation and alienation. We heal the feelings of estrangement that produce pain, hurt, anger, and even violence. When we feel alienated from anyone, that sense of separation seeps into all areas of our lives. We can't feel as prosperous, secure, and happy.

When we engender a sense of gratitude for belonging to one another, we no longer have those feelings of being a stranger in an alien world so often. We begin to see that each of us is a silken thread of flesh and bone in a magnificent tapestry that exists in the mind of God. We allow the Master Artist to create a work of art by saying yes to being woven with one another in a dance of beauty, appreciation, and peace.

When we pray in gratitude for our relationship with God, when we say yes to a kind of belonging that joins us with all others as a part of the family of man, the resources of the universe rush to bless us. We experience the miracle of freedom and joy that a sense of belonging brings.

Each Sunday I begin the service by sharing an inspirational quote about the power of love, of which gratitude is an expression. Then I ask people to stand and share a sign of God's love that lives in them with one another in greeting. People get up and reach out hands to one another. Maybe the greeting is as simple as "Good morning." I go out into the congregation myself and what I hear are happy, vibrant voices mostly saying things like, "How are you? I'm glad to see you." Or, "Great to see you. You look fabulous." What I see is a lot of people with huge, bright smiles on their faces. I see people hugging. And I feel a palpable shift in the energy. It comes alive because people are enlivened. I think it's because we experience the truth that we are one. We feel again the sense of belonging that is so easily lost or forgotten in a world where people are living stressed and disconnected lives.

The more I practice gratitude in these four ways, the more I have faith in God, others, and myself. I don't get so stressed over the unsavory appearances and experiences in my life. Praise God! It's as if something opens in me that is otherwise closed. I am able to rise above any negativity or aloneness I feel, out of my petty judgments. Life becomes meaningful and worthwhile. It's as if the ore of my life is alchemized into gold. I know beyond the shadow of a doubt that this practice will change your life forever for the better as well. Gift yourself with this practice and you will be gifting the whole world.

Practices

- Close your eyes and breathe deeply. With each breath, imagine that you are breathing in pulsating white light from the infinite resources of God. Breathing this way, go back in time, recalling the many good things that have happened in your life. Remember your successes, all of the good deeds you have done, the kindnesses you've given. Recall special events, happy moments. Count these blessings, naming them one by one. Notice how you feel. Breathe and feel a sense of appreciation for yourself and the Divine in you that inspired it all. Anchor in your heart any good feelings that come. Then notice the outlook you now bring into your day.

- Any time you think of a miracle that you're wishing and hoping for, start thanking God for it as if it were here now. Give thanks in advance for the good you seek.

- Remember to make a gratitude list each morning before leaving the house and end your day with a gratitude list before you get into bed. Taking nothing for granted, count your blessings. Then notice the good experiences in your day. See if they don't increase.

- You can never say "Thank you, God" too much. Make a commitment to increase the level of your thanksgiving. Take time to notice the quality of your life and your days as you do this.

- As you think of any difficulty you're experiencing, instead of becoming anxious or complaining, give thanks for the blessing in it.

Affirmations:

I give thanks to God for all my good, and my good multiplies.

I give thanks for all that I have, and all that I desire comes to me.

I give thanks for the blessing in the problem, and the problem becomes a blessing.

I give thanks for belonging, and my sense of belonging expands and deepens.

My life is beautiful.

Prayers

The psalms are a great place to find ideas for expressing thanks and praising God's benevolent activity in our lives.

You have turned for me my mourning into dancing; you have put off my sackcloth and clothed me with gladness, to the end that my glory may sing praise to you and not be silent. O Lord my god, I will give thanks to You forever.

—*Psalm 30*

It is good to give thanks to the Lord and to sing praises to Your name, O Most High; to declare Your loving kindness in the morning and your faithfulness every night . . . for You, Lord, have made me glad through Your work. . . .
—*Psalm 92*

Bless the Lord, O my soul, and all that is within me; bless His holy name. Bless the Lord, O my soul, and forget not all His benefits, who forgives all your mistakes, who heals all your diseases, who redeems your life from the pit, who crowns you with steadfast love and mercy, who satisfies you with good as long as you live so that your youth is renewed like an eagle's. —*Psalm 103*

God, thank You for being the joy that turns things around for me. For all the times I've been down and remembered to turn to You and been lifted to hope, thank You.

Lord, I give thanks that whenever I turn to You, You are there as some sense of peace and hope. You are there to guide me when I am confused. You are there to help me forgive even when I don't want to. Your love breaks through the walls of fear and sets me free to dare to follow my dreams. Thank You for Your Presence in me that is greater than any fear.

Dear God, thank You for the joy I feel and the love I can now express where before I hid in my self-imposed safety.

Dear God, thank You for all of the good in my day. Thank You for helping me in all the difficult circumstances when I have no idea what to do to make things better. Thank You for my friends and for the people I work with. Thank You for the little inspirations that come throughout my day.

Closing Thoughts:
Embodying Your Prayers

Prayer is always only a thought away. In any moment a thought turned Godward takes you into the fourth dimension of existence—the realm of the sacred and the infinite creative power of the Divine. It will minister to you right where you are for just what you need.

Let your life be your art studio and design center for prayer. Step up to the canvas of each day with your palette of prayers and know that you will create an authentic work of art with any of the beautiful colors and textures of prayer thoughts that you apply. You can intensify the color according to your need.

My prayer is that you will continue your discovery of the peerless creative power of prayer, savoring at the end of each day the ways your soul has been fed and your life enhanced by the artisan of prayer that you are becoming. It is an adventure for a lifetime.

Selected Bibliography

Amidon, Elias and Roberts, Elizabeth. *Prayers for a Thousand Years*. San Francisco: HarperCollins, 1999

Evely, Louis. *Our Prayer*. Oxford: Mowbray, 1975 (Originally: *Le Priered'un Homme Moderne*, Paris: Editions de Seuil, 1969 and copyrighted in 1970 by Herder and Herder, Inc.)

Templeton, John Marks, ed. *Worldwide Worship*. Pennsylvania: Templeton Foundation Press, 2000.

Loder, Ted. *Guerrillas of Grace*. Philadelphia: Innisfree Press Inc., 1984.

Mosley, Glenn, and Joanna Hill. *The Power of Prayer Around the World*. Pennsylvania: Templeton foundation Press, 2000.

Nouwen, Henri. *The Way of the Heart*. London: Darton, Longman & Todd Ltd., 1999.

Oman, Maggie, ed. *Prayers for Healing*, Berkeley: Conari Press, 1997.

REVEREND SHARON CONNORS is a senior minister at Unity Village Chapel at the wprld headquarters for Unity in suburban Kansas City, Missouri. She has previously ministered in churches in San Francisco, California, and Gainsville, Florida. Prior to ministry, Sharon worked in management training. She has been an adult educator, high school counselor, and Spanish teacher.

Contact the author at.
    Unity Village Chapel
    1901 NW Blue Parkway
    Unity Village, MO 64065
    (816) 251-3590

or
    prayerfrontiers@yahoo.com.

Silent Unity

Silent Unity is a beacon of spiritual light that shines prayer into any personal darkness. It is a welcoming voice asking, "How may we pray with you?" The voice that answers your call responds to your need in a way that inspires hope and instills a sense of peace.

For over one hundred years the Silent Unity prayer ministry has been serving people of all faiths from all around the world. Silent Unity workers are available twenty-four hours a day, seven days a week. You may call Silent Unity (1-800-669-7729) to receive the spiritual strength of prayer support. Prayer requests may also be submitted online at www.unityworldhq.org.